LOST HEARTS

BY THE SAME AUTHOR

THE HAPPINESS BOOK
ALL IN A DAY'S WORK
ETON VOICES
THE CATHEDRAL
THE NOBLE TRADITION

LOST HEARTS

Talking about Divorce

Danny Danziger

BLOOMSBURY

First published 1992

Bloomsbury Publishing Ltd,
2 Soho Square, London W1V 5DE

A CIP catalogue record for this book
is available from the British Library

ISBN 07475 1268X

Printed in Great Britain by Clay Ltd, St Ives plc

AUTHOR'S NOTE

The people I have interviewed for my book are real people. I have changed their names, and the names of their spouses and children. They have talked to me knowing the destination of the interviews – for which I am extremely grateful.

CONTENTS

DIANA

He said to me, 'Who are your ten favourite modern novelists?' which is rather a conversation-stopper, actually, and certainly not terribly seductive . . .

For some reason I was hell-bent on getting married, I was always getting engaged, I'd been engaged to three different people.

But I had just broken up with somebody, and so there was nobody special in my life, and I was sharing a flat with my sister. And I went to a party and Harry was there, and we chatted away, and I thought he was rather marvellous-looking, he had this wonderful, vulpine, Celtic face, blue eyes and black hair and very good bone-structure. He was very much my type of good looks.

And he drove me home in his Jensen sports car, which in those days seemed like a glamorous car, and he came in and had a cup of tea.

When we kissed goodbye, he somehow realised I wasn't wearing a bra, I remember I was wearing a cashmere, V-neck, cream-coloured jumper so it was quite evident, and he jumped three feet backwards, which I thought was kind of strange; instead of being turned on or pursuing anything, he just seemed horrified, as if he had touched a hot coal. So off he went back to Holland Park, and I heard no more.

I thought: I must do something to see this chap again.

I was working in a design agency, and I was the toast of the agency in a way because I was young and pretty and rather good at copy-writing. And there was something called the creative lunch, which meant that every month somebody in the creative department organised a speaker, and then you took them out to lunch, and it was my turn, so I thought: I will ask Harry because he is a writer, and everybody is always writing a novel in their office. And he came and gave a brilliant speech, which he did totally off the cuff, and he said, 'Let's not have lunch, let's have dinner,' mainly, I think, because he didn't like going out to lunch, not because he was romantically interested.

He said he would like to go to Park's, which in those days was the most expensive restaurant in London. And then my mother rang up on the day we had arranged this date to give me her tickets to see Paul Scofield in John Osborne's play *A Patriot for Me*. And after the play Harry stood up and screeched, 'Bravo,' which seemed rather unEnglish – and I thought that was marvellous, I think it is terrific to show one's emotions and pleasure so fearlessly.

And then he and I went off to dinner which was pretty awful; Park's was famous for garnishing dishes with chrysanthemums and things like that, but it all seemed a bit weary, the chrysanthemums were gravy-stained, as if they had done their time on another dish, and neither of us thought it very good. And the bill came to £10 which in 1967 seemed like a fortune.

Also, it hadn't gone terribly well. He said to me, 'Who are your ten favourite modern novelists?' which is rather a conversation-stopper, actually, and certainly not terribly seductive. I just couldn't think of anyone at all, and I knew that whatever I said it would be wrong. Finally I spat out, 'Carson McCullers,' whereupon he said, 'She's dead.' It was all a bit like that. He just isn't a very good conversationalist. But I decided to ignore that because he seemed so dashing and successful and handsome and dynamic.

And again I didn't hear from him after that.

So I asked him to a dinner party, and I cooked rather well and in a style he liked, very non-Park's kind of food, and after this dinner party he started ringing me up at the agency, and this is very Harry-like, he'd say, 'Let's meet at your flat and have a bite to eat,' so of course that meant that I had to produce food: but I'd do it brilliantly in about ten minutes, I'd make a really good purée of flageolets with something grilled, it was all quite clever for those days and for somebody my age, and I think that got to him, and I really was very pretty too.

And his friends must have said she seems a good thing, and he invited me to his cottage in Yorkshire, he had a cottage in the Yorkshire Dales, and I thought: I've cracked it.

So I went off on this weekend, and it was awful, it is a long way to drive, and he barely spoke at all, also, he made me buy all the food and then didn't offer to pay for it, which I thought was fearfully mean.

I remember just feeling bored and embarrassed, and awkward, not sure what I was supposed to do; he wrote all the time, hundreds of pages, and I cooked and washed up, I just didn't know what to do. I remember asking once, 'Would you like me to dust?'

It was the first time we slept together, and it was terribly ordinary really; it wasn't that he couldn't get it up or anything, it was just ordinary, ordinary and perfunctory. And I remember we woke up in the morning, and I have always thought mornings much sexier than evenings, and he jumped out of bed and started brushing his teeth, there was a basin by the bed, and I was still half asleep, and he flicked cold water on me – sort of why don't you get up and boil an egg or something, whereas I was thinking: When you wake up you fuck and kiss and cuddle, but he just flicked me with cold water. There again I could have taken my cue and run, but I didn't.

It was summer, and we went for a long sweaty walk and came to a pool, a natural pool, and we took our clothes off and jumped in this icy cold water, and when we got out he dried himself on my shirt . . . I mean there are a million signs all along the way why this man was probably not ideal material, but I ignored all of them.

I do remember coming back from this very silent weekend where we barely spoke and ringing my sister and saying what a ghastly, awful time I'd had. But nothing deterred me, I went on and on.

I used to go round to his flat and cook: he never took me out to meals which I would complain about. And then on my birthday he took me to a restaurant in Chelsea which no longer exists and it was all quite romantic, I thought, but he spent the whole evening absolutely riveted to the conversation of other people at the table next to me, and I remember being very put out by that.

We went to Kenya for a holiday that summer. It was a lovely holiday, Kenya was unfashionable then, but we had some nice times, except I got ill, I was feeling absolutely ghastly with some sort of stomach upset. But Harry went out for the whole day to lie on a beach and have a nice time, leaving me to the mercies of the people running the hotel, and I remember thinking that was a bit mean. A doctor was summoned who came and stared at me, like any man might, finding a woman lying by herself in a hotel room.

But it got more romantic on this holiday, 'I love you's and so on, and, in a rather romantic place called Malandi, he started talking about how he wanted to have children, from which I inferred he meant with me, although it wasn't put quite like that. But he was by this time 34/35, he was getting on – he was twelve years older than me, and I suspected he was quite keen to get married and have children.

Anyway, when we got back we started living together. And then he said to stop using any contraception, so I did, and I think I got pregnant that very night, I feel sure I did, because nine months later I had David. Once he knew I was pregnant he said let's get married.

We went out to dinner, this was the third time in three years we'd been to a restaurant, and we went to one in Camden Town, which is still going, extraordinarily enough – and whenever I have been there I have been sick afterwards, including that time. And we sat down and he said, 'Now, who can we invite to the wedding . . .' And he got out a pencil and paper and started listing all his famous friends, well-known writers, and I just burst into tears because I wanted to talk about life and hopes and fears, and children, not sit down and make a list of all the literati we could invite to the wedding. I piped up and said, 'I have some friends too and I want them to come,' so then I was allowed a grudging little list of my friends, none of whom was famous enough.

We went to Austria for our honeymoon where Harry fell off a horse immediately and hurt his back, and that wasn't much fun because there was no sex as his back hurt too much. And anyway, when I got pregnant he wasn't very keen on sex; sex was always drab really, all a bit functional, and I think very much aimed at procreation.

Right from the word go we had this terribly middle-aged marriage. I was only 24, but I stopped working at that point, and it was jolly lonely because I had left my friends and my job, and Harry would bound out of the house very early in the morning to go to his club to write, and come back really late, and I would spend all day thinking what I was going to make for dinner.

David was born in the September and Harry went absolutely wild about David, he was over the moon, and everyone said they had never known Harry be so enraptured by anything, he couldn't concentrate, he couldn't write, he was just entranced by having produced this baby, and his enthusiasms and affections were all for David. And I felt very excluded, so that didn't get things off to a good start.

And then we had Liz and then Edward, and I got terribly depressed, and I remember our doctor coming round, who said to Harry, 'Do you have to come home at seven at night, do you do a job that means you couldn't come home a bit earlier?' And I remember thinking: God, he's absolutely right, I had been brainwashed into this idea that Harry had to write twelve hours a day, and that writing was the most important thing.

He looked a bit discomforted and admitted that perhaps he didn't have to come home every night at 7p.m., but it didn't stop him, he never came home any earlier.

We had a big party on my 30th birthday, and I remember thinking that everyone else was enjoying this party much more than I was. And it was soon after that I went to another party and started chatting away to a theatre director called Justin Orde, and began having an affair with him soon after. We went out to lunch a few times, and he said let's go back to my flat . . . I was horrified by my behaviour. Having an affair had never occurred to me as an option, I felt very married with three kids who were small, and I felt very wicked and dreadful, and I went home that night and I couldn't sleep. But he really did wake me up in a sexual sense, I mean he was frightfully keen on women and a good lover and very funny and nice to be with, I hadn't ever had that sort of fun, it was just wonderful, he made me come alive and enjoy what I had never enjoyed, which was that feeling of my own sexuality and my own prettiness.

And soon after I started having an affair with him I started having an affair with somebody else which became a much more major event. Justin was rather skilled at having affairs and keeping his marriage, he had it all worked out; Jonathan jumped in just as enthusiastically as I wanted to because, in those days and probably still now, when I met somebody I wanted to captivate them completely and be everything to them and them for me, I have a very babyish idea really about relationships.

When Harry found out about Jonathan, he immediately had an

affair, which he let me know about, but I have also discovered since he had plenty of other bits on the side. Harry was having affairs and not letting them impinge, whereas I was having love affairs and wanting them to impinge.

And we then lived in a sort of arrangement whereby we 'did our own thing', we would be able to have affairs, we would be able to sleep with other people, but we would go on with the marriage, and with the children.

It was one of those let's have an open marriage, kind of thing, and of course it doesn't work, well, it didn't work for us, and we started going to see a therapist. It was the first time that either of us had been to see anyone like that, and Harry and I sat down opposite Desmond Pelly who is very authoritative-looking, and in a rather odd way looks like Harry physically, and Harry started saying, '. . . and she does this and she does that, can you imagine, blah blah blah,' and at the end of this diatribe Desmond Pelly looked at him and said, 'Christ, if I was married to you I would do just the same.' And I remember looking in the mirror when we got home and ten years had fallen off my face, I mean all this terrible guilt I had been carrying around had all been alleviated. And Harry looked absolutely ashen-grey, he couldn't believe that another man would betray his own sex with a remark like that.

The marriage seemed to drag on and on and got worse and worse, and I stopped seeing Jonathan, and started an affair with someone who was a lot younger than me, a student, which went on for years; it was a convenient affair because it didn't get too much in the way of my marriage, it was mostly letter-writing and the odd week away.

Harry meanwhile met the woman he has now married.

It all would have gone ahead fairly amicably if he hadn't suddenly inherited two million pounds whilst we were still married, and I thought: Well, since we are still married and he's got two million pounds he can jolly well give some of it to me, and so that ended up very acrimoniously, and I cease to exist for him now.

I just wish I had known the effect it would have on the children, because I would have worked a lot harder keeping it together in some guise. Harry very much wanted to.

I have just started analysis and I am now quite content.

I have a boyfriend, and we have a very volatile relationship where I am trying to preserve various areas of independence; I can't say he is Prince Charming, part of the analysis, I think, is to be more the person who would attract Prince Charming.

MALCOLM

One night we went round to my friends Simon and Penny to babysit, and it must have been the merest trickle of sperm got inside her, I think we were lying almost fully clothed on the floor, engaging in what at the very best was an exploratory fiddle so goodness knows how . . . Sarah Jane must have had an extraordinary capacity for getting pregnant . . .

I'm surprised I haven't been married more, because I am very very keen on marrying, and I use the idea of getting married as a chat-up line, and I endeavour to seduce people by producing little marriage scenarios. The first night I say, 'Hey, wouldn't it be amazing if we got married, and did this . . .' and I produce little images and fantasies of the flat, and if the other person plays the part it's hardly surprising that I fall into it myself.

And the real marriages have occurred for really rather different reasons. I mean the first marriage to Sarah Jane Gwendolen Rosamond Glastonbury, that was a typical late-fifties marriage – because she was pregnant. There were only about four men at this college where we met, and there were about two hundred women, so the shop window was stuffed full of sweets. And they were all southern women, they all had polite accents. My friend Tom and I both had northern girlfriends we finished with as soon as we came across these sweet-smelling, smooth-skinned, two-car Surrey people, we were overwhelmed with lust. Playing the working-class card was just about coming in, the Finneys and the Courtenays were riding high, and we could be as rude and vulgar as we wanted and still do quite well. Sarah Jane had nice, big eyes, somebody said later she suffered from ophthalmic goitre, but anyway, she had big tits, and she was regarded as rather cuddly and sweet, not the best catch in the place but all right, and several fellas were chasing around after her. I shared a room with my mate James Wilmot, and he was after her as well, so there was a bit of competition between us, and I think the fact that there was some competition made her more attractive.

And one night we went round to my friends Simon and Penny to babysit, and it must have been the merest trickle of sperm got inside her, I think we were lying almost fully clothed on the floor, engaging in what at the very best was an exploratory fiddle, so goodness knows how . . . Sarah Jane must have had an extraordinary capacity for getting pregnant. It really is a cautionary tale.

She got expelled from the college, those were the days being pregnant meant that you were morally beyond the pale.

You couldn't get an abortion then. I remember some crude attempts to try to abort her myself, banging her stomach, trying to get some pills; we'd heard vaguely that there were people in Switzerland who did abortions, but I didn't have a clue how to do anything about that.

So I married her because she was pregnant.

I had to go and tell her mother. Her mother was a headmistress of a kindergarten school, and she was absolutely stuffed with ideas of rectitude and moral propriety, I mean you could not possibly imagine anybody who would relish less the prospect of her daughter being pregnant out of marriage. And I remember going over to the tiny maisonette her mother lived in, and telling her, and her mother, who was rather given to histrionics, throwing herself against the wall, and then collapsing in a faint on the floor.

I didn't know anything about my wife whatsoever. It was only gradually that I found out what sort of person she was, and she was an extraordinary woman, I mean a very, very obsessive, strange woman in many ways.

Well, you see, Sarah Jane looked plump, Sarah Jane looked nice and cheery, at school she had appeared rather like everybody else, quite a cheerful, bright-eyed woman. But I discovered that really she was extraordinarily disturbed in a whole variety of ways.

In the small flat her mother had brought up Sarah Jane, on the wall was a great big chart in which she had to recall all the number of times she went to the toilet, whether she had been, as they called it in the house, properly, or whether she had urinated, and she had to put ticks to indicate when she had been. One of the first things I discovered about Sarah Jane was that she was absolutely agitated about lavatories and toilets and urinating. She couldn't go to the theatre, because she was obsessed by the fact that there were people in the theatre who wanted to have a piss, but couldn't get up and go.

The cinema was a bit easier, because of course people can get up in a cinema.

She couldn't deal with changing our son's nappies, she couldn't face the smell of shit, or anything connected with that, so I had to do it, there was no question of sharing it. And she hated Jack the first few years because she couldn't cope with all of that.

Leaving the house, she would always say something like, 'Do you want to go to the loo?' And I would say, 'No.' And she would say, 'Are you sure?' I would say, '*No, I don't want to go to the loo.*'

The second thing: Sarah Jane was anorexic. I didn't know what anorexia was, the word wasn't in common use then, but this meant not only she didn't eat, but, like all anorexics do, she fed me, she fed me enormous amounts of food – I have got pictures of myself at the time in which I am something like sixteen and a half stone – while she would sit with a little bit of cottage cheese on a plate and wouldn't eat anything. And the result was that she was continuously ill, I mean her hair was always dropping out, she had terrible trouble with her fingernails, and she had no periods.

When I got my degree we moved to Derby, which is a dreadful place, and then on to Exeter because I got a job there. And she followed me around, just tagging on really, she didn't have any life of her own I now realise, and that must have been pretty terrible.

Our arguments were violent and vicious, and we shouted in public at each other, we took a certain delight in the fact that people were shocked and amazed at how we went on, perhaps there was a certain rather perverse delight that we could take afterwards. That was a developing aspect of our relationship, there were certain perverse areas around which we could develop little fantasies. All that toilet stuff: I could be out in the car and say to her, 'All right, I feel like a piss now.' And she'd say, 'No, no, no, you don't – do you . . .?' and I'd say, 'Yes, I do . . .' And this, I realised, could develop into something she could become a little bit sexually excited about: it was an area of such tortured concern to her, but it was also a sexual arousal thing for her, I mean she could then become aroused and fancy the idea of sex.

In a way we were locked together in an unholy alliance: even though we didn't really like each other very much, there was a certain perverse eroticism between us which sustained us. Later on, I saw all these 'golden showers' adverts, and you realise that quite a few people are obsessed, I suppose as a result of particularly strict toilet training, and anything which is a taboo area can be implicated in sexual arousal.

I was faithful, I was absolutely faithful, because in the same way that abortions were something that other people did, affairs were something other people had.

But there wasn't much sex, hardly any. Indeed, I remember going away for a weekend to my friend Mick, and I had an idea Mick might be trying to fuck Sarah Jane, and I used to leave them together, I'd half allowed myself to believe they might be having a fuck, and although there was a sort of male concern: how dare my mate do this? I know that I routinely went to bed early because I had a little sense in my head that I wouldn't mind if it did happen – because by that time I had lost all interest.

It wasn't until I got to Exeter and it was the sixties I suddenly realised that I could leave, that there was more out there, there was better out there. Suddenly, the possibilities that I didn't need to go on living like this for the rest of my life began to occur.

Psychologists often talk about getting permission to do something, you suddenly realise you're allowed to have some.

I can remember exactly the first thing that happened. In one of my tutorial groups there was a woman called Francesca. She looked a bit like Julie Driscoll, tight little hair-curls and little leather miniskirt, all that sort of gear was *de rigueur*. I can remember feeling she was the most intelligent woman in the group, and then having some sort of conversation with her. *She* suggested we have a drink. And then she said, 'Why do you have to look like you look?' I said, 'What do you mean?' She said, 'You're so fat, why don't you get some jeans or something?'

And then Francesca said, 'Why don't we go for a drive?' I'd bought one of those sit-up Renault cars, a very conventional, safe, family car for a university lecturer.

I said, 'Where?' She said, 'Just drive.' 'Well, where do we stay?' 'Stay where we stop, we sleep in the car, whatever.' So we went off. We drove and drove and drove, and we went to Ayot St Lawrence for some reason, maybe she was interested in Shaw, perhaps I knew something about Shaw, I don't remember.

And when we came back, we went to her house, and she put on a record as we lay on a mattress on the floor of her bedroom, and then, rather clumsily, that was my first little affair. Of course, I immediately decided I was in love with her, I was absolutely overwhelmed after these perverse years, after all these very strange years, after all these anorexic years, no periods, dislike of Jack, the arguments, the shouting, this was amazing.

But then she chucked me, and went off with some muscular second year, and I was devastated. I just wandered around getting totally drunk, lying in gutters in the middle of Exeter. Once again, permission had been granted to have dramas and behave badly and not be happy with your wife, and be in love, all these types of over-emotionalisms were occurring to me everywhere.

And then, seven years after marrying Sarah Jane, I persuaded her that it would be a good idea to go off and do a degree, and so she went off to university.

And then I suggested it would be a good idea if we separated, which we did.

The divorce was something like five years after we had separated. We hadn't had much to do with each other, just discussions over what was happening about Jack. Sarah Jane came up from London to Bristol where we were going to get divorced. I can remember being in the courtroom when Sarah Jane was on the stand, that incredible eroticism when you see the person you have known terribly well in that strangely alien setting.

I suddenly wanted to go to bed with her. As I say, it was a thing which was always founded on perversity, so what could be more deliciously perverse than having got divorced to go and have a really good fuck at the Mayfair Hotel in the centre of Bristol. And she knew it as well, I mean she was wicked in a way, and we could easily fire each other off with this perversity. So we came out of court and I said, 'Have you had anything to eat?' and typically she'd come all the way from London that morning and had had nothing to eat. So we went to this seedy snack bar, maybe there are only seedy snack bars in Bristol, and she said she'd have cheesecake. I remembered she'd always liked cheesecake. So she had a piece of cheesecake and a coffee. And I watched her as she put her fork up against the pastry, it was a crusted cheesecake, and she managed to pull whatever there was of the cheesy part of the cake away from the encrusting pastry, move the pastry to one side, and then just eat the inside. And I suddenly thought: No, that's absolutely completely useless, I couldn't have got it up, that particular anorexic, neurotic behaviour was something I remembered drove me mad. So we disentangled and she went back to London. It was perversity which drove us to the possibility, but it was this other little perversity that made it impossible.

I was really caught up now by the idea of falling in love and finding the perfect woman, and a whole lot of people came into my life. I then met a woman called Kate Williams, and I lived with her for four years, but then Kate went off to Bristol – people were always going off to Bristol in my life – and she finished with me, she chucked me, which was terribly sad. We had talked about marriage a bit, but she hadn't been very interested, she hadn't fallen for that old line.

Having lost Kate I was looking for somebody like Kate again, but before that there was Marina, which was another gross error.

As a result of the late-sixties, the early-seventies, I got involved in politics. We used to meet at the local pub, all us working-class boys were going to have the Revolution. The place was full of middle-class women, and we all played more uncouth than we were; of course you had to get drunk, and women had to be fucked – we were all Jack Kerouac or Leary or whoever we were, and there were a lot of laughs, and demonstrations to go on.

I was getting a bit of a reputation because I was doing a bit of television and writing for the *Guardian*, I wrote a few 'We are all liberated now and forward with the revolution'. I was just one among a very large number of lefty, trendy academics, but provincial really, stuck in Exeter.

And I had a succession of women living in the flat, Kate was followed by Kate Orton and Juliette Harris, I could give you a list of twenty, thirty names, two or three women a week, but then I met Marina.

She was very beautiful. I mean Marina had curly red hair, and she had all these beautiful southern manners, I mean Marina was upper middle class, her father was at that time head of an enormous public company. They had a house in Mayfair and a big house in the country, and Marina had made a name for herself, she had appeared in photographs all over the national press standing in her miniskirt with her gorgeous red hair. I mean everyone had heard of Marina Harington, she was a catch.

I got a phone call from her saying she'd read one of my articles and wanted to talk about it.

I thought this was a bit of a come-on really. Anyway, I met her in the Coach and Horses in Soho, it was about the only pub I knew in

London. Then we went to what used to be Bianchi's opposite Scott's, and at the end of the meal we had about five grappas each, went back to her flat in Pimlico, sat on the bean bags and talked. I was just about to go when she asked, 'What sign are you?' And I said I was Aquarius, and it turned out she was Libra, and Aquarius and Libra go together, and we somehow as a result of that laughingly managed to get into bed together, so that was the start of the Marina thing.

Now that seemed to me absolutely wonderful because here I was newly arriving on the London scene, and she knew people, she could introduce me to people. She had some quite classy friends, I mean one of her friends was Julie Christie, for example; Ralph Steadman drew a picture of me, and I remember when Marina first saw it she said, 'It doesn't look like you, take it back . . .' I said, 'I can't go back to Steadman and say it doesn't look like me . . .' But she made me do it, and I went back – and he stuck a bolt through the neck, that was the only addition he made.

It was good fun, it was always good fun, and we always amused each other, I think we still do. I was a lout really, a bit of a hooligan, but now I was going out with a very refined, sophisticated, subtle, southern, well-known, beautiful feminist. She had no hangups, there was nothing that worried her, she loved her parents, she loved her job, sex was normal and natural, she could talk openly about private functions, I can't think of anything neurotic whatsoever about Marina, she had all the uncomplicated clarity of the upper middle-class southern Protestant, and the fact that she was now a feminist had more to do with the times in which she grew up rather than any internal ideological necessity – but she would be outraged to hear me say that . . .

It's a nice antithesis to the previous occasion, because we got married because she wasn't pregnant. She did get pregnant, but of course she simply rang her doctor friend, and he rang up a private clinic. I then met her at the Expresso coffee bar in the Portobello Road, and I asked, 'Is everything all right?' and she said, 'Yes, fine,' she had had the abortion. I could see she was upset, and I said, 'But you are upset, aren't you?' And she said, 'Well, I suppose I could have had the child and we could have been together,' and then, something about somebody being brave, this sudden vulnerability, I think that was what precipitated it, and I said,

'Well, I think perhaps we should get married, don't you?'

So we got married and I invited every old girlfriend, everybody from the past I could possibly think of. Her father paid for it all, it cost thousands and thousands of pounds.

Her family were an appalling load of snobs who found it very difficult mixing with my family.

At the wedding, the two families had nothing whatsoever to do with each other, my family were just stuck sitting in chairs in the big room, and all her family were in the private bar drinking champagne, it was outrageous. She said, 'Oh, it's just father, he's an old fascist.' But her father *was* an old fascist, the peculiar capacity of these upper-class girls to have a fascist father, but not to worry about it '. . . but Daddy's always been like that.' She used to talk about it as being funny.

Marina couldn't stand my parents, she couldn't disguise how appalled she was. She could have coped with the working class, she had a notion of the working class, I think she rather looked forward to meeting the working class on behalf of whom she was doing so much. But because my parents were lower middle class they had certain pretentions, but they couldn't really live up to them: my mother serves salads with dinner, but her salads consist of a lettuce leaf with a whole tomato in the middle of it. Being confronted by these semblances of her own life, she was appalled by them. She could manage a pint of bitter or a bottle of brown ale, but she was totally unable to drink a Waitrose Riesling. It's a complicated thing.

And then it began to go wrong fairly soon, in rather gentle ways at first. I suppose the first thing was that we argued. They were intellectual arguments. With Sarah Jane there had always been emotional arguments, she was suspicious of theory and suspicious of academics, but Marina used to have the same argument, we used to call it the D.H. Lawrence argument in which she would say, 'D.H. Lawrence is absolutely appalling and one shouldn't read D.H. Lawrence.' So I said, 'What do you mean D.H. Lawrence is absolutely appalling?' 'Well, his sexist attitudes. . .' I said, 'D.H. Lawrence was exploring the boundaries of sexuality, he may have got some things wrong but he was extraordinarily brave for his day . . .' 'No, no, he was a sexist.' Now it sounds ridiculous, but we could have that argument, the D.H. Lawrence argument or some version of it, for an hour, two hours, fairly regularly.

The second thing was dinner parties. She liked the idea of dinner parties. I tried my best. But the lower middle-class pub culture was still fairly strong, and I always liked the idea that at night you went out, whereas Marina thought you had nice friends round and you prepared a beautiful meal and sat and drank fine wine and had a conversation. I didn't like all those couples arriving round, I was never very good at dinner parties, and I began to develop what I am now certain was a psychosomatic thing, I began to get this sinusitis, I would say, 'I can't breathe properly,' and I had to go out. I was always rubbing my temples and would drink cups of hot tea to deal with this sinusitis.

I was still teaching full-time in Exeter, so I would get up at five o'clock on a Monday morning and drive all the way to Exeter and come back up again. But I was beginning to have affairs in Exeter. I had been behaving badly, I was up there five days a week, and there were lots of opportunities, there was no AIDS around, or anything like that.

I had two or three running at the same time with people who were the complete antithesis to Marina. I can remember I had an affair with a woman called Pat McGraw, who was a postgraduate, she was one of those really scruffy, bedraggled, roll-your-own, spotty, slightly smelly sort of hippy chicks, she really was rough. But she was funny, and of course she was the perfect foil to Marina. Where Marina has never appeared in anything other than clean knickers all her life, Pat might or might not have knickers on, or if she had they would be greasy, and the bed she slept in was revolting, and the kitchen stank, and she had this horrible dog, but she was funny, she was really marvellously funny, and she could make me laugh, and she could make me laugh about Marina.

The idea of sex as a straightforward, rationalistic function, a bit like a private dinner party really, was impossible, and this in a way had messed up sex between myself and Marina because there wasn't anything of that sort of thing, none of this little secrecy.

For example, Marina could smoke dope as though it was the most reasonable thing in the world to do, but the trouble is, a tiny sort of illegal *frisson* needs to accompany it to make it worthwhile, and with Marina it didn't have any of those accretions. It was something you did, rather like sex was something you did, like dinner parties were something you did. She sanitised everything . . . everything was normalised, everything was rationalised.

At first I thought I liked it tremendously, because, after Sarah Jane, it was clear, it was open, there were no hidden depths, no perversity.

I was nearly caught on a couple of occasions, and eventually I had to confess to one of them, and that was all right. But it was a very cruel moment when I decided it really was all over, it was impossible.

What happened was one night I was lying in bed, and Marina was undressing to get into bed, getting into bed in a very businesslike way, taking her clothes off, folding them. I can remember sex wasn't going at all well, possibly because Pat and I had managed to get a little bit of perversity going. Pat loved those stories at the back of *Mayfair* where people said, '. . . and then I . . .' These stories were always '. . . and then I took my clothes off', or '. . . and then I saw her nipples were erect'. She used to get me to read the 'and then I' stories to her. Now the possibility of getting a copy of *Mayfair* and reading a letter from the back of it to Marina was absolutely, utterly impossible, Marina would want to say, 'But this is a sexist magazine.'

Eventually Marina said, 'But why aren't we having sex?' and I said, 'There's just not enough excitement.' But I thought: Excitement depends on something I can't imagine having with you, I mean your version of sex is one that somehow can never be exciting to me.

She went out and bought Alex Comfort's *The Joy of Sex* and brought this book back and said, 'Well, perhaps we could use *this*,' and it said something about how a little bit of S & M can often invigorate jaded sex lives. And one night I went about tying Marina on the bed, tying her wrists and her ankles to the bedhead – the book said, 'This will then be arousing . . .'

And I can remember Marina dutifully lying there with the notion that this was going to reanimate our sex lives, and thinking this was absolutely ludicrous, and how humiliating to subject Marina to this.

And I just felt absolutely overwhelmed, here she was trying to reinvigorate our sex life by agreeing to do this because a book had led her to believe that this was the way to reinvigorate it, but it was just ridiculous.

I had been corrupted by being with Pat McGraw. With Marina there was never going to be that eroticism, it was straightforwardly sexually satisfying at its best, but it never contained that edge of eroticism which I needed. After a time you begin to learn about yourself and to recognise your sexuality. I needed to be surrounded by these notions of being covert, being secret, being whispered, being guilty, being in the corner, being slightly perverse, being this, being that, and really the last person on earth who needed to get entangled with someone who believes that is somebody like Marina. She was much more sexually liberated than I was, she could talk about it readily and easily in a way that would embarrass me. But under the clothes with Pat or Sarah Jane I could whisper things that I could never possibly whisper to Marina . . .

We were in bed about four o'clock one morning, and she said to me, 'We've got to talk about the fact that we're not having sex any more, will you please tell me exactly what it is?' And I said, 'All right, I don't fancy you any more . . .' It was a terrible thing to say, and I've said to her since, 'I'm sorry, I didn't mean it,' and in a way I didn't mean it, it was not that she wasn't attractive, but there wasn't that sexual *frisson*, and I couldn't explain that to her – because it was something she wouldn't recognise, or in the activity of recognising would rationalise in such a way that it would disappear.

And when I said that she packed her bags and went down to the station at five o'clock in the morning, and that was it, we were then divorced.

I don't think much about Marina, I go out with her for meals from time to time, and I sit there and think how beautiful she is, and I like her voice, and her teeth, and how clean she is, and how well brought up. But then after about two hours, she says something, possibly about the Labour Party, and she has notions of what other people want, that she, Marina and her class, can work out the best way for organising the world, and the world should be pretty grateful to them for having organised it in that way, and it's useless.

SHELLEY-ANN

I started to run fourteen miles a week, they say when you're sexually frustrated that is what you do . . .

I was at school with Hugh, so I had known him all my life. We had interests together, we painted together, and became very good friends.

And when he asked me to marry him, I was 19, 20, and I'd never been out with anybody else. I was totally devoted to him, and so we got married.

We spent a month on Lake Geneva for our honeymoon, but things were just not right, and the marriage was not consummated: he wouldn't sleep with me, and we had no sexual relationship at all. And the whole relationship began to deteriorate straight after we got back.

We moved to his parents' house and we lived with his parents. He would never listen to me, it was always what his mother said, I never felt I was his wife because he only paid attention to her.

He hated his father, probably motivated by his mother who at that time was in her late-50s; my father-in-law was a good twenty years older than her, but extremely virile, and sometimes she would come to the breakfast table, and she would scream and cry, 'He crawled over me all last night, he crawled all over me . . .'

His sister was extremely intelligent, but suffered from manic depression. One day the most appalling scene took place shortly after I had moved in to their home. I don't know why, but she came over and screamed, 'You're a bitch, I hate you . . . he's *my* brother,' as if she was having an incestuous relationship with her own brother. She once cut her wrists after one of these outbursts.

I painted the guest bedroom pink, and thought: Hopefully we will have a baby in there . . . but nothing was said about children.

I wondered why two single beds were going upstairs, surely if we're married we must have a double bed, but two single beds were put into the house.

He then started to masturbate on his own – he wouldn't allow me to touch him – once, twice, three times or four times a week, sometimes in front of me, sometimes in the bathroom, and that upset me so much I went to the doctor. I didn't understand what was happening. I asked the doctor, 'Is there something wrong with *me*?'

I thought I liked sex, but I didn't know much about it, I was a virgin.

I started to run fourteen miles a week, they say when you're sexually frustrated that is what you do.

And then I thought: This is foolishness, I'll have to find out about things, so I went to New York with my husband on a business trip, and I had an affair, in a very calculated way, to find out exactly what sex was like. Of course I had never had an orgasm before . . . and it was wonderful, the greatest thing that ever happened to me, and I found out that I was a normal woman.

Please do not misunderstand me, I'm not a nymphomaniac, but sex is very important in a relationship, and if you don't have it, it's soul-destroying.

Meanwhile I had to go back and deal with the situation of living in this relationship, of being terribly unhappy and frustrated.

I went to doctors, I went to the church, I tried every avenue to make the relationship work because I loved him very much; but it wasn't enough, I obviously didn't do enough.

When I went to see a psychiatrist, she said, 'You should call a divorce lawyer now.'

But I said, 'No, I'm not ready to hand in the towel yet.' I had gone through all this pain and agony, and I would not give up because I loved him very much – and I was not going to let the mother-in-law have the better of the situation.

I took a lover. I couldn't stand it any more, and then a proper relationship started with a wonderful man who was a proper man, who was a helicopter pilot in the Air Force, the most macho man that you could find, the complete and utter opposite to Hugh, and he hauled me out of that appalling situation, and gave me the will to live. And I was very happy with him.

I have cried and I have had much remorse. Hugh has seen the pain

I had because our relationship didn't work, because I loved him, I loved him very deeply.

But I have now been told by friends that Hugh is a homosexual . . . that he likes little boys. He is dying of leukaemia, they say; maybe he has AIDS.

In a funny way I still love him, but I have put him out of my mind now.

I'm very much happier now I'm 40, I'm my own woman. With my husband I gave my whole life, my soul, my body, the whole of me. But when you're 40, you realise you don't have to give the whole shop away, you may have a liaison with a man, but you don't give him everything.

The man who pulled me out of my marriage was divine, I was crazy about him, I loved him. Sadly, he is now going blind with diabetes, and sexual relations for the past two years have started to diminish – and he won't marry me. I respect him enormously for not marrying me and putting me through another ordeal in my life.

But when will I get the happy ending?

REBECCA

I was used to men who are persistently ambivalent about marriage . . . because you are supposed to be a grown-up, independent kind of woman, you don't leap up from behind sofas with engagement rings – but actually, you'd rather like it if they did want to marry you . . .

He turned up in my aerobics class, and I thought he was a bit of a fool, but quelled this, because he was an extremely nice, terribly enthusiastic sort of person.

He was the class clown. When asked to do exercises, he would make comments – not with a particular degree of wit, he would make funny noises and things, while everyone else was just getting on with it. He also enjoyed playing the clown at a party, which I didn't mind to begin with, because it is very nice to have somebody who is so unselfconscious they don't mind if they look a fool.

The first few dates were an enormous laugh, a tremendous amount of giggles, and that was a terrific relief. He really could in the initial stages make me laugh, and that's the biggest aphrodisiac known to womankind. And enormous generosity: 'You want the ceiling painted, I will paint the ceiling.' 'You want *that* fixed, I'll fix it.' He was very much a person who whisked into your life and took over, he would come to the flat Sunday afternoon, and say, 'I can mend that, we'll do it now.'

He used to say, 'Stand back, all my work is guaranteed for forty-five minutes,' which I thought was quite funny the first time I heard the line, until I realised that actually was more or less the truth of it; if a set of shelves was put up, it was a question of waiting for them to fall down, and if he installed a telephone, a month or two later, British Telecom would be round saying, '*Who* did this?!'

But initially it was very nice. I hate doing all those kinds of things, Black and Decker frightens me silly. And when you are single, and you have been single for a very long time, which indeed I had, I was well into my 30s, it's bliss for someone to take practical things away from you. I was reaching a point in my single life when if somebody would reach up and change the light bulb, it was a gift from heaven.

My life felt a mess, a big mess. I'd let everything drift, I'd ended one unsuccessful relationship that had gone on for four years, I'd never had a relationship come to fruition in terms of marriage, and I felt very much that I should have. At weddings – one had obviously by that time been to a lot of other people's weddings, they didn't say, When is it your turn? they said, 'What a pity she didn't . . .' and you are beginning to feel a freak.

Marriage was mentioned on the third date; he was playing the fool in a pub, rather a strange pub in Norfolk, where there isn't a bar, and people sing. And there was a singsong going on, which is the sort of thing at which he excelled, and which, apart from lack of competence, is the sort of thing I absolutely loathe, and he went down on bended knee in front of the whole audience in the pub, and to roaring cheers turned the line of song into a proposal. I took it in the joky spirit it was intended, and simply said, 'Don't be a bloody fool.' That got a cheer too, and quite a few boos, but of course it stuck in the air, and having said it, he just went on repeating it. It became a standing joke, he would say to people in groups, 'I keep asking her to marry me but she won't, you know.'

It was very embarrassing, but one can't but be rather taken over by this kind of declaration. It was the lack of ambivalence: 'I want to marry you.' I was used to men who are persistently ambivalent about marriage, and about their relationships, and because you are supposed to be a grown-up, independent kind of woman, you don't leap up from behind sofas with engagement rings – but actually, you'd rather like it if they did want to marry you.

For a moment I was getting increasingly confident that he was the one, but quite quickly I came to realise that I couldn't live with this man when suddenly all the jokes and all the things that had made me scream with laughter were on about their fifteenth recycling, and I realised that he had a vocabulary of about fifteen words . . . he was very very limited. But he loved me to pieces, and that is a very seductive state of affairs, you can almost love somebody for loving you.

But I knew he was wrong, I said, 'This absolutely won't work, it just won't work.' So he went off to work abroad.

And while he was abroad he wrote to me. It did coincide with a point in my life where I was just heartily sick of being on my own, and managing on my own. There were various awful things going on in my life at the time, like my mother getting Alzheimer's disease, and suddenly, I don't know, absence making the heart grow fonder, I thought: Well, why not, for God's sake? I am sure you can overcome these irritations: this person about whom you have got reservations, he has got no reservations about you, and you don't half need a right arm. And I thought: I don't have a great deal of respect for your intelligence, but I can think for both of us, you just be the right arm and do the practical things.

So he came back from working abroad and he proposed the night he got back, in my living-room, and I accepted.

I went to sleep that night thinking: Oh God, you fool, you fool, how are you going to get out of this?

But I did it all the same. We set the date for ten days later. I went through the next ten days in a state of complete and utter hell.

I told some friends at work who found me sort of scrunched up in the corner in my office, getting thinner by the minute, sobbing. The one who was single said if you really feel this strongly, you mustn't do it. The one who was long married said everybody has pre-wedding nerves, and so did my sister, who was also married. It was as if the married people wanted you to join their club. And, of course, there is a bit of you that hates to make a public display, so you wipe the tears sooner than you probably should, and you cut back on the explanations of how desperate you really feel, and pretend it's all OK.

I did try to tell Edmond, but I was rather cowardly about it. I said, 'Are you sure this is right . . .?' but his reaction was so extreme: 'What do you mean, for God's sake, you can't do this to me . . .' that I would immediately back off, I couldn't bear the confrontation.

It was a cowardice that got me into the registry office, zombie-like, desperate, but gritting my teeth, and I was relieved to get that bit over.

The honeymoon was a complete débâcle, we argued throughout, it was desperately, desperately unsuccessful from every single conceivable point of view. The first night we stayed in a very nice inn near Melksham in Wiltshire, a beautiful inn, one of the nicest places I can ever remember staying in. And it was a very hot night, the window was open, and a large black cat came and sat on the bed. It was terrifying at first waking up and seeing this soft moving object at the bottom of the bed. And I thought: This is an omen. I thought: Life can't get any worse than this, lying like a poker, wishing he was a million miles away.

Sex was dreadful, it was virtually nonexistent: it has to be said he had great problems in that direction anyway. In the year that we were married we probably managed it successfully three times. He would just about get it up, but that was it, as soon as it was supposed to do anything, everything would kind of fade away. And that sets in a chain reaction, an expectation of failure, which becomes an intolerable burden. To begin with I would pretend I was enjoying whatever there was. I was pretending so that I wouldn't hurt his feelings, but I wasn't kidding myself. You get sick of saying, 'Don't worry, it doesn't matter, we can try again another time . . .'

Every one of the odds was against it working – background, approach to life, intellect, sex – it had nothing going for it. And I did it, and I shall to my dying day wonder why.

As part of the honeymoon we went to South Africa where we managed to make each other totally miserable for two and a half weeks. We had quite a lot of late nights with friends and fellow expatriates, and if we were with other people it was fine, he would revert to the *bonhomie* and the heartiness, but everything went rapidly downhill as soon as we were on our own, we had absolutely nothing to say. It was a Jekyll and Hyde situation. There was this bag of laughs in public, and this complete wimp in private.

His *bonhomie* faded and there were no more jokes, and he then became extremely crestfallen, because I think he very quickly realised that he had taken on rather more than he could deal with. And he immediately became completely subservient to me. 'Anything *you* want.' 'Should we turn left or right? You say.' And I was made very much to feel the absolute centre of his existence, and that I was to guide him through every single thing.

We settled into my flat and began married life together. It was the equivalent of an emotional haemorrhage. Very soon I was like a person being put through the shredder, I looked very thin and drawn, run down, I had great difficulty in sleeping, I was drinking too much, smoking too much, I was a bag of nerves really.

We were slightly saved by one of my brothers who came to lodge with us, a rather vulnerable younger brother, who one didn't want to upset; he didn't actually know what was going on, but the presence of another person saved us from a great public eruption. But in private we were incredibly tense, and in bed we couldn't bear to touch one another.

Then I found myself at the doctor's. I couldn't bring myself to say, I'm living with somebody I can't bear, which is driving me up the wall – coming home in the evenings, I walk around the block fifteen times rather than open that door. I just said, 'Would you please give me something to make me sleep?' And he said, 'I don't think that is what you want, I'll just give you six.' And I got to the top of the road and thought: You know bloody well what you've got to do. Why are you asking for pills? And I put them in the wastepaper bin, and went home and said, 'I just can't stand this. This is my flat, and I'm afraid you'll have to go, so you'd better start looking for somewhere else.'

He was angry, but he couldn't ever bring himself to raise his voice to me, or to tell me he thought I was being a complete and utter bitch. You see, he absolutely couldn't ever face up to me. I think I was capable of terrifying him, I only had to snap or to say anything unkind, and he would be desperately wounded. And he would never talk about the fact that this marriage was disastrous. He would always say, 'Look, it takes time to adjust, you're not giving it a chance.' I said, 'I would give it a chance if I thought we'd have something fantastic at the end of it, but we won't, we'll never be able to talk to one another. If we both worked incredibly hard, it would be at best a convenient arrangement of two people living together, and it's not worth the struggle for that.'

He didn't really reply. He said, 'If you insist, that's what I've got to do.' I took off for a fortnight, and I said, 'I think it would be better if you were gone by the time I come back.' It felt brutal doing it, but I was the one giving the orders all the time. The only way to cope with Edmond was to say, 'Go in that direction and do that,' and he would do it, there was no way he was going to resolve this mess or even face up to it by himself.

I went by myself to a cottage which belongs to a friend, I felt like a convalescent, but I was already feeling better, having made the decision.

I immediately put the flat on the market, which was another way of underlining things to him; apart from anything else, I absolutely hated it, it was a ghastly flat. When you're in the vein of making wrong decisions, you make them all wrong. Having made the wrong decision to marry him, and having married him, I then went out and bought the wrong flat, in the wrong place, and filled it with the wrong furniture. Luckily it was a time when the market was very bullish, I was able to sell it quickly. I said to him, 'Well, you could have been buying a flat by yourself, I think I owe you something.' And he said, 'I wouldn't take a penny piece off you, I wouldn't dream of it,' which very rapidly turned around to, 'All right, how much are you going to give me?' So really out of guilt, I paid him quite a lot of money which enabled him to buy his own flat, which made me feel better, but a bit of me hated him for taking it. But I could see why he did.

Once he was established in a flat of his own, that's when I began to truly recover, I could see that actually I hadn't done him great damage, and I felt better about myself.

We preserved the fiction that we were friends but we couldn't get on in the married state, which he wanted to believe. I was determined I was not going to let myself say, I can't stand the sight of you, although by that time I did dislike him hugely.

He is a person who is absolutely loyal and reliable: if you break down on the motorway in the middle of the night, he is the one who would come out and fetch you, all of that.

But in a sense he was incredibly dishonest about himself. In his case it wasn't a conscious dishonesty, it's not like somebody telling you a lie knowing it's a lie, it was a long, slow, almost lifelong process of self-deception. It's the sort of thing you see on the witness stand in a courtroom: the best liars are the ones who have convinced themselves they are telling the truth. He was dishonest about what he was doing for a living, the way he represented it to me.

He was a person who was always playing a role. He had represented himself as a kind of consultant, and he represented himself as much more entrepreneurial than he was, much more important than he was.

He implied he was better educated than he was – I shouldn't have been fooled for a minute. He could pick up things from the newspaper, and quote what other people had said, and give himself the veneer of a person who constantly discussed theatre or the arts. It was his coming in and picking up a book and saying, 'Oh, this is a good author,' giving me the impression that he had read books by that person. I don't think Edmond had read a book in his life. He wanted to be the kind of person that read books.

I think one of the worst things about divorce is that it is a colossal knock to your self-esteem; I spent a year feeling like a leper, full of self-hatred for being such a fool, for having caused such a mess, and in the course of that year I didn't particularly want to go out or see anybody, and my libido hit rock bottom. No matter how liberal and grown-up you think you are, and how forgiving you would be to someone else in that situation, you can't be anywhere near as forgiving to yourself, even though the logical part of your mind is saying that this is the most difficult thing in life to get right, and you shouldn't hate yourself for having fallen at the first fence.

ROB

There were four seagulls.

No, there weren't, there were five.

No, four.

Five.

And then I would feel my heart beating, thumping, pounding.

Four.

No, five . . .

I met Amanda at university almost as soon as I got up there; she was older than me, she was a year ahead. I had one quick fling, and then started going out with her for the rest of the time.

I think I just fancied her legs at a party, so it was lust that first drew me to her.

She thought I was a cocky little upstart, she didn't like me at first. But I got her drunk, and on our first sexual encounter, we made whoopee all night, which was fun; when we came to repeat it a night or two later, sober, we both felt a bit inhibited, cack-handed, we went through the motions, but it didn't happen. Then the third time, there was an awareness that it might not – which is what happened, and very quickly sex became a problem, and we ended up not wanting to go to bed with each other.

There was a lot of sexual tension and uncertainty. We had an awful sex life to start with.

I don't know why. I was turned on by her, I was able to go through the physical act, and yet, although on paper the right results occurred, given points out of twenty, it didn't score very highly. It was as if we were doing something against the odds in a curious sort of way.

We started to say let's not bother with it – we won't have sex for two weeks, say, and perhaps it will remove this tension for a while.

Meanwhile, we became an established couple, it was Rob and Amanda, we got invited everywhere as a couple, and were seen as such by everyone. But at university the temptations to have a go with someone else are very strong, and I think we both did once or twice secretly.

She left a year before me, she went down to London while I stayed up there for another year – for another two years, as it happened, because I failed all my exams: I had not attended any lectures, and I was drinking too much.

And so we conducted a postal affair, telephoned each other, wrote occasionally, she came up once or twice, and I would go down to London, and at that stage sex became very bad again. She discovered about some girl I had slept with, a friend of mine told her. I am not sure really what made us persevere with it, and I can't for the life of me think why we ever got married . . .

I had great fun after she left, there were a number of women who I knew fancied me, and with them I had much better sex. I am quite lascivious, I like dirty sex, I am not very good at loving embraces full of meaning and spiritual significance, I like sex with people I don't know particularly well. But at the same time I could never take anyone else very seriously, my emotional commitment was still with Amanda, and one or two of these girls, I know, were quite badly hurt, and I was not far, I should think, from seeming very cold and callous.

When I finally left university, Amanda had already got a flat in Clapham and I went and lived with her. I didn't like London, I didn't have a job, and I remember feeling very insecure, I definitely felt left behind. Amanda had got a job with some film company, she had a busy social life, and I felt like a man tagging on; and so I suppose I was very difficult to live with, I became quite short-tempered and irritable. And sex wasn't good again.

When the lease expired on the place we were living in, by then we had been together in one form or another for five years, and we decided to buy a house, it seemed sensible, and so we got married in order not to upset anyone. I think she put it to me: 'If we are going to buy a house, oughtn't we to get married?' And I said, 'Yes, I suppose so.' I can distinctly remember not being joyful about it, and not being sad either, it was just my life.

I made one romantic gesture when it was all decided, I went out and bought her a ring for far more money than I could afford, and I took her out to dinner and presented it. It went down very well, it was a nice ring, she was happy.

And then we booked a cheap honeymoon because we didn't have much money; she wanted to go to the sun, and the only place we could afford was Tunisia, which is a hideous place, for a start, and we were in a horrible new resort. I was absolutely bored to tears for two weeks, there wasn't another English soul to speak to or sit with in the bar, and Amanda just lay in the sun covered in body oil, and read horrendous novels from the beginning of the time to the end, while I wandered around the swimming pool trying to talk to people. I would have liked to have gone on a walking holiday or have had something to occupy me. We had been together too long to canoodle for two weeks.

And then we became occupied with the business of doing up the house; we did one up, and then we moved as soon as we'd done that, and did another.

I was beginning to get tired, I was running my business, doing flats up in the evenings and weekends, and I was physically exhausted, and I became very ill.

Amanda was away, she had been in the States a lot, working for the film company, so she wasn't around when I went to my doctor. I said, 'I keep getting these terrible pains and dizzy spells, I can't catch my breath,' and he said, 'Well, have you tried eating more breakfast?' And I said, 'There must be something more serious wrong with me, I am blacking out virtually . . . Am I going to die?' And I went to another GP, and he said, 'Listen, your breathing rate is terrible, and you're hyperventilating which is making you giddy, you are very stressed. Have you talked about your problems?' 'What problems? I haven't got any problems . . .' 'I think you should see a psychiatrist.' I said I would think about it. So I went home, and it was the night of the General Election, and I went to vote at the polling station. And, as I came out of the polling booth, my head started to swim, I began sweating, and I got this terrible heart flutter, and I really thought my number was up. I became filled with an incredible feeling of fear, raw, naked fear, I was terrified. I slumped against the wall, and I couldn't breathe, I couldn't move. Somehow I managed to stagger back to the house, and I stayed up all that night, I was like an animal in a cage, I couldn't sort my head out, and for three years I was ill, badly ill, I became barely able to function.

I then went to a psychiatrist in Harley Street, and he was a useless old buffer. For five or six sessions he never said anything, all he'd do was sit vacantly and stare at me, and I needed to know, was I sane or was I insane? I was getting awful, terrible fears, I would see a programme on television, or read a book, and they would conjure up chains of thought and fears that I dare not speak of to you, strange, irrational, sexual fears.

Amanda came back, but I was incapable of having sex, we had been having bad sex anyway over the previous months. Amanda had not been particularly interested in sex since getting married.

The whole psychology of it became very complex; I was thinking: On the one hand, she is not interested, so it's her fault, so I can't be held responsible. And then I would think: Well, the reason she doesn't want sex is that I am making no endeavour to make her feel wanted, I am putting her off sex subconsciously – or deliberately – by my attitude towards her, so it *is* my fault. You go round in vicious circles, and it gets very hard to establish any kind of truth. But, whatever the truth was, we didn't have any sex, and at that stage I really couldn't have cared less, it was the last thing on my mind.

I would be driving along the road, and there would be, say, some seagulls on a wall. And I would drive past and I would say to myself:

There were four seagulls.

No, there weren't, there were five.

No, four.

Five.

And then I would feel my heart beating, thumping, pounding.

Four.

No, five.

What if I don't find out how many there were?

And I would have to drive back and count them. Almost anything would trigger off this incredible panic response. My frame of mind was such that I was always saying to myself: What if . . .

What if I am a homosexual?

Maybe this is all because I am a homosexual, and I haven't come out of the closet. I've got to come out.

But, Rob, you are not a homosexual.

You are a completely screwed up homosexual, you can't even fancy a man because you have suppressed it so heavily.

And so it would go on, my thought-processes at the time were mightily destructive.

But I went to work every day, I was running my own company and making decisions, and that's what kept me sane, actually, because they were decisions I was still able to make; my employees may have thought: Rob doesn't seem to concentrate, but I managed to go out and do estimates and sell, and that in a way saved me.

Towards the end, I was going to the psychiatrist for my appointment, and I somehow went to the wrong bloody place. I sat down in the waiting room and I was in an inpatients' clinic. There were people in pyjamas milling around, going 'Er, er, er,' drooling, shouting, completely fucking ga-ga, and I thought: I am no better than this. I was sitting there, shaking like a leaf, locked in fear. And then I thought: This is the end of the road for me, this is the lowest moment, and I became incredibly angry with Amanda for not knowing half of what was going on, she wasn't even in the country at the time.

And when she came back, I said, 'Listen, we have got to divorce, we can't go on,' and she knew that I was unbalanced, and she didn't know whether to say, No, Rob, we must ride it out. I had the upper hand morally because I was sick, I could dictate the terms. But maybe that's a complete misconception because she undoubtedly must have wanted out. She was having a bad time, there was no sex, I was half bonkers, and meanwhile she was having a serious flirtation, affair, maybe, I don't know to this day, with her boss at work. I don't really care either way. Did I know? Did I suspect before I had my breakdown? Was it responsible for the breakdown? I don't know. If you'd asked me was Amanda having an affair with her boss, I would have said probably not. I would imagine they had got to the point of knowing their desires and intentions, and I would guess that they hadn't actually slept with each other at the time.

We went for a walk and stopped at a tea shop, and agreed that we would separate. She was going away to America again for a couple of months anyway. And we would sell the house. It was sad, but not desperately, I had too many other problems as well . . . That's a curious thing to say when you are getting divorced – that you have got too many other problems as well, but there are problems and there are problems. It was a positive move to try and sort out what was already a mess – looked at like that, it wasn't such a terrible thing.

I felt positively relieved by this decision. The house sold very quickly, almost instantly, while she was away, and I never saw her again. It was over. It wasn't something I wanted to resume or pick up, it wasn't as if I had thought: When I get my head sorted out, then I will go back to her, it was: Thank God that nightmare is over.

It was very easy, very simple. I petitioned on the grounds of irreconcilable breakdown, and we were divorced within two or three years, decree absolute.

There were a couple of phone calls. News reached me about a year later that she had moved in with her boss. Now she's married him.

My health remained bad for another year, some say I am still not well . . .

MOLL

I looked at that horrible mouth that used to kiss me, and those horrible teeth he never used to brush, except once a week he'd clean them with Vim, and those horrible hands, with those horrible big sausages on the end of his arms, he was disgusting . . .

Alan had come up from London, he was a hippy, he had long hair and a beard, and was really grown-up-looking; everyone I knew then looked like a boy.

He came in to my mum's chip shop where I used to work after school, and on weekends – and for no money, I wish to make it known, and I thought he was really nice, I had a real crush, and I used to trail him about, like a kid really. I just wanted to be with him, and I did want him to love me, and fancy me. He seemed kind of unobtainable because he was 24 and of course he didn't really want to go out with a 15-year-old girl . . .

He probably thought I was attractive, this was a very small village, and I was probably the most physically attractive girl around. I had very long hair and I used to wear fantastic clothes, I'd bought my own clothes, second-hand, for years, because my mum never used to buy me clothes, and I'd learned how to look good and I was very tall. I was quite sophisticated because my mother believes in independence – total neglect – so I could cook a bit, not brilliantly, but better than my mum, and I could sew. My parents had each had two marriages, and I suppose that makes you a bit grown-up. So I did probably appear quite independent and grown-up for my age.

We'd go for walks and hold hands. I suppose we kissed and that sort of stuff, snogging. Then we went to the Ely Pop Festival, and he had a sleeping bag which he slept in, while I slept in a potato sack. On the second night he said I could share his sleeping bag, and then we had sex . . .

He wasn't very sexy; it didn't take very long, and even though I was only 15 I had this feeling that perhaps it was meant to go on a bit longer than five minutes. I asked, 'Can you do it again?' and he'd say, 'No, because I'll have sperm on me, and you'll get pregnant.'

Then I started going out with him.

I was very unhappy at home as my mother was very aggressive: she's lovely now, she's a really sweet, harmless, doddery nit, but she was very aggressive then, she was unhappy, she'd married this bloke she didn't love, she was pregnant, which was the last thing she wanted to be at 37, and she was just thinking she'd thrown her life away. And she used to take it out on me a lot.

So we decided to run away from home on my next birthday . . .

Every day at school I used to block in the calendar towards the day when I was going to be 16.

And then I changed my mind. About Christmastime, I thought: I don't love Alan. So I told him, 'I don't love you, I think we ought to split up.' And he was incredibly upset, he cried for hours. I'd never made a man cry before and I felt really responsible and guilty. And so I said, 'I didn't mean it, I'm really sorry, I do want to stay with you after all,' because I pitied him.

That night we had sex, and he said, 'I'm going to get you pregnant.' And of course I was then instantly pregnant, because you're something like 98 per cent fertile when you're 15.

I remember when I told him, he was pleased because he had knobbled me, bastard . . .

So then I thought: We'd better run away sooner than we planned. Also I was frightened because my mum was becoming very violent, she was always hitting me – and I was afraid that I was going to fall down the stairs and hurt the baby, I became really obsessed with my well-being when I was pregnant.

And so we brought it forward by a month to the 4th of March, which was a Saturday. I said I was going shopping in Swindon, and we ran away to London on the train. I cried the whole journey.

I loved my mum, you know, you do, even when she's horrible to you.

We went to live with Alan's ex-girlfriend, Patricia, and her boyfriend called Nick Barlow, who was a burglar. She was a kind of posh nosh, and he was her bit of rough, as Alan had been – but he was like real rough.

Then we went on holiday, me, Alan, Nick and Patricia. Nick was on the run, he'd jumped bail or something, and he stole this red Volkswagen beetle. We went up to Wales, and then on the way back we went through a village called Llewan and passed a pink house on a bridge which had a little sign outside saying 'Flats to let, apply within'. So we stopped the car and applied within. It was a small house, and the four of us lived together. Nick used to beat Patricia up, it was horrible. She would have black eyes and be in a right state. But she kind of asked for it, I know that sounds awful, but it really did look like she wanted him to do it, she used to wind him up, and I could see he was going to beat her if she didn't stop . . . He was a vicious bastard.

And then they couldn't bear living in Wales any longer so they moved back to London, leaving us behind.

And around about that time Alan started to get violent. It would often be over sex. When I was about four or five months pregnant I got very sexy, I wanted to have sex all the time, and he didn't at all. And so I used to cry, which often led to him hitting me. Then he would be sorry. In a way it seemed kind of dramatic and romantic, you know, somebody hits you and then they say sorry, it wouldn't now.

He couldn't have sex without fantasies. He would ask me to describe what my schoolfriends looked like without clothes on, or he'd say, 'I'd really like to fuck you and your mother at the same time,' and all that kind of stuff, which I used to find thrilling before my orgasm, and really horrible and upsetting afterwards, but I went along with him.

For years, I couldn't have sex unless the person I was having sex with was fantasising about another woman.

We got married when I was 16. He said, 'If you don't marry me I'm going to leave you,' and I'd just had Gordon, he wasn't six weeks old, so I had no choice. He said, 'We've got to get married, otherwise your mum's going to take me to court and do me for statutory rape and abducting a minor.' He was frightened of that.

We didn't know anyone except local people, the people in the shops, and they were very sweet but they were old, so I didn't really have any friends until I went to college – I wanted to do my O levels, and I did them in four months. That made Alan very aggressive, because he felt inadequate.

I remember once asking him, 'Could you take Gordon out for a walk because I'm revising for my history O level,' and he smashed me, pulped me. He was very clever, I would never have a black eye or bruises which showed; sometimes he used to hit me on the legs, but usually he would hit me all over the head so that it would be under my hair, he was very premeditated about the way he used to do it.

He began making me have sex with him which by now I certainly didn't want. He used to knee me in the kidneys if I said no.

Either I would be completely floppy, or I'd be completely stiff, like rigor mortis. He used to be disgusting, absolutely disgusting. He'd take out his big white donger, it always used to be a bit dribbly, and he'd sort of dip it in my vagina to get it wet, then he'd push it in – and it seemed enormous – until he had an orgasm, and I used to feel every shudder, every contraction, every squelch, every squirt, every drop inside me. While his head was buried in the pillow next to me I would make a silent scream.

I don't know what was my breaking point. One day I just thought: What the hell am I doing here?

I rang my mum. My stepfather had died, which was awful, not that she was loving to him, they fought all the time, but she wanted somebody there, which was rather convenient for me.

He used to ring once a week, used to beg me to go back, he said pathetic things like, 'Please come back, I'll buy you a vacuum cleaner . . .'

I lived with my mum a whole year just so that I was protected from him, because he was scared of my mother.

And then I didn't see him again until Gordon was 16. At Christmas he rang up and said, 'Can I come and see Gordon?' and I said, reluctantly, 'Yes, OK, you can come . . .' I didn't like it, I felt uncomfortable, I hadn't seen him for years, and it was a shock to actually have him in my house. And I looked at that horrible mouth that used to kiss me, and those horrible teeth he never used to brush, except once a week he'd clean them with Vim, and those horrible hands, with those horrible big sausages on the end of his arms, he was disgusting.

He just wouldn't leave, he was swigging back the gin and tonics, he was stabbing his great big sausages into the nuts and helping himself to everything. And just seeing him reminded me, it was as if he'd just hit me, as if he'd just raped me, last week, yesterday. It was very bizarre. I woke up on Christmas Day and I was crying, I was really upset. And my husband, Will, said, 'For heaven's sake, it was sixteen years ago, can't you forgive and forget?' and I said, 'No, I can't.' Mum was here, my mum who's very unaffectionate and unphysical, and I actually went and got into bed with my mum, crying. And she cuddled me, saying, 'The bastard, the bastard . . . I didn't realise he was such a bastard.' I said '. . . then he did this, Mum . . . and then he asked me to talk about you in bed, Mum, it was terrible.' Then I forgot it again. I don't think Will, I don't think anyone can really understand what it felt like.

Although obviously I love Gordon, I'm thrilled with Gordon, I needed to have Gordon in some ways, on the other hand, it's swings and roundabouts, I think I could have done lots of things, but I just didn't get around to doing them.

BEATRICE

His great drawback as a husband was that he was an absolutely chronic philanderer . . .

My adolescence was not spangled with wonderful romantic affairs, I wasn't at all successful with boys. I think I was rather priggish and bookish, I wouldn't have fallen in love with me. But here was somebody who was head over heels in love with me, and I was terribly excited about this, and I was also extremely excited by the fact that I absolutely loved his family, he had quite a lot of brothers and sisters, and they were wonderful to me. My own mother is very beautiful and artistic – and frustrated, she was not an easy mother to have, and I suddenly found there was a lovely cosy mother all ready and waiting for me.

I have a feeling I was probably more in love with all of that than I was with Anthony. I don't think I was ever actually in love with Anthony.

We met at university. Undergraduates go around in herds, and we shared a great many friends, so in a way our own relationship was hardly progressing, because you are distracted by this permanent cocktail party that seems to be going on, even at eleven in the morning over cups of coffee.

I think I was rather afraid of him. He was a bully really, and because I was scared of him I didn't make scenes about endless drunken nights with the lads, playing bridge and drinking port, and then being revolting to be with the next day, or quite a lot of flirtations with other girls, even though he was committed to me.

Sex wasn't at all successful. We didn't know what we were doing really. We were both virgins, and there was a great deal of rather incompetent muddling about, but it wasn't consummated until our honeymoon – would you believe you could do anything so idiotic, it's all I can do not to shove my daughters at people to stop this happening.

He proposed at a Christmas dance; it was a very successful dance, everyone was tremendously happy, and in an impulsive moment he suddenly said, 'Will you marry me?' and I remember a great feeling of relief, because I saw that as an answer to what to do next, because I had never been encouraged to have a career.

But I do remember afterwards an absolute panic about being engaged, and looking at girls on the train who weren't wearing engagement rings, and being sick with envy.

Looking back, I am so ashamed I ever allowed the thing to happen, the feebleness of it all . . .

We got married nearly a year after we came down. It would have been our silver wedding this year, which I had entirely forgotten, until my first mother-in-law pointed it out the other day.

The wedding was very pretty and very conventional, there were about three hundred people, and I was in quite a state all the wedding morning. I felt sick and miserable. And then, after the reception, we went off to Portugal for our honeymoon, and I cried all the way there, I nearly drowned Anthony, I should think, I cried absolutely solidly. My mother had left a present in the bottom of my suitcase, a bottle of the scent I use, and when I saw that I was completely beside myself.

In a funny, schoolchildish sort of way our honeymoon was rather fun, there was quite a lot of larking about, and we laughed a lot. It was the last time we laughed.

Sex was not something we coped with very well, followed by my feeling: Well, this is clearly something I am not very good at, which was a feeling that persisted for a very long time. And Anthony thought there must be something more to this, and went off to find it.

His great drawback as a husband was that he was an absolutely chronic philanderer.

All he did was sow the wild oats that are entirely natural for a young man to sow in his 20s, but he sowed them after marriage rather than before, and it was absolute misery to live with, and I got in a frightful state about it, but looking back I have a great deal of sympathy for him.

We had a flat in London, and very soon we bought a house in Midhurst, I can't quite think why we did anything so dull, I think we were still being nudged by our parents to do tidy and conventional things. And then I became pregnant with Emma, and at that point Anthony went to America on his first business trip, and that is when the serious straying began. It was his first lovely expense-account whirl abroad, and I think he took full advantage of it, I mean he was a healthy, red-blooded young man of 23.

You always know about these things; if you are a victim of infidelity there is a smell in the air, there is something highly charged in the atmosphere, I think the betrayed one, man or woman, has a nose for it.

I felt terrified and tremendously inadequate, then I simply made my mind up to not be any good at sex, and I tried not to think about it. I mean Anthony had sex with me, he was very urgent, and I did often feel turned on, but nothing happened. There is a world of difference between having sex with somebody and making love to them.

Anthony was fundamentally afraid of me, I think he sensed that for all my surface vulnerability I was quite clever, I was slightly too clever and perceptive for his peace of mind, and philandering was one way of keeping me down, to keep me in a kind of knife-edge nervous state. And so he wasn't somebody I could trust, and sex needs a bit of trust.

He wouldn't like to see me as successful as I am now if I was still his wife, that would be a threat: writing was only right while it was a kind of hobby that could be stopped.

When we were alone, it was then that the relationship was at its most formal, because there were strict parameters of conversation and discussion, the children, his career – we talked about him and his career, which began to flower very quickly, and we talked about that absolutely eternally. There were certain things about my life that he felt were acceptable to talk about, but one couldn't discuss people, he had very strong feelings that family and friends were not up for analysis as characters, and there was no human discussion. It meant shutting down on any topic that became too personal.

For a banker's wife in those days, there was an enormous amount of entertaining to be done, and one was always on parade looking perfect, and he liked the fact that I looked OK, and I was articulate, but I must never never overstep the mark – be too clever.

He increasingly wanted me to appear urbane and international and polished. I remember we had to do a business trip to Gleneagles with some huge American industrialists, and we went in a private Lear jet. I was terribly excited by this, and I remember him begging me not to tell them that I had never been in a private jet before. And I disobeyed, and I said to the chairman, 'Could I go and look at all the dials with the pilot?' And he was charming, and said of course I could, and Anthony was very angry about that, he thought the naivety was sickening.

The awful thing is that I never confronted Anthony. We had confrontations about one big affair, and another affair he had with a great friend of mine – who is still a great friend of mine – I don't think she knows I know. And Anthony would always say, 'I really won't do it again, I am never going to be unfaithful,' and within three months, bingo.

I was withdrawing further and further from reality, and it manifested itself in truly ghastly nightmares and sleepwalking. I think I was as close to being round the bend as I will ever be, nightmares and sleepwalking make you doubt reality, they unhinge you. I would find myself in various parts of the house absolutely unaware of how I got there.

My subconscious was saying that my marriage to Anthony could not go on, but I simply could not think what to do about it. Of course, looking back, I should have left, and I should have done it years before, but it didn't strike me until terribly late on that I could leave this relationship.

Then I met Andrew. And I felt that I had come home, I suddenly saw how a relationship could be – and it was a complete revelation. To be with a man who hadn't been to public school, who liked women, who was not afraid of women, who didn't mind talking about his feelings.

I met him in November, and I told Anthony I was leaving him the next April. And I said I was leaving him not to have an affair, but because I wanted a proper marriage. And in those five months, everything that had been awful about being married to Anthony became clear to me, it was taking the lid off Pandora's Box, and I couldn't stop seeing all the monsters then.

Anthony tried frightening me, as he always had, only this time it took the form of shouting and screaming and telling me he had ways of making me stay his wife. There were ludicrous scenes. Then it took the form of toadying to me. We had this trip to the Far East, and every time I walked into the hotel room, there was another fucking bunch of roses. I can remember wrenching open the window of the Mandarin Hotel in Hong Kong, and hurling them out the window.

He could not believe he had lost. He said he loved me, he said he wanted me to stay, but I think he didn't want me to win, and he didn't want Andrew to win. He knew that I had not only found a husband, but I'd found a lover, and he couldn't bear that.

I stopped sleeping with him. I just said I wasn't going to have it any more. And that was when I began to realise he was actually rather cowardly, that when I stood up to him he crumpled; he crumpled about Andrew, he crumpled about sex, and I suddenly found, after seventeen years of doing what I was told, I was suddenly calling all the shots.

But it was wonderful, it was like being let out of a cage, it was extraordinary to realise I had the strength.

You can't have a long relationship that comes undone without grief for it, its ending has to be worked through, and it gets worked through in your subconscious. I found I dreamt about Anthony quite a lot. I had periods of feeling terribly unsettled, I would feel tearful and ill at ease. And the first year with Andrew was really quite hard emotionally, the surface water got a bit choppy – the deep water was always fine, and I knew that I'd done absolutely the right thing, but it was hung about with difficulties.

Anthony and I have a very amicable relationship now, but it's distant, and it's really only to talk about the children. He is a very good father to the girls, but he is a party-time father, they go to him for fun – lunch at the Connaught is with Daddy, but if you have got a migraine and your boyfriend has just chucked you, you come home to Mummy and Andrew. He's married again, for the fourth time, to the kind of girl he's always admired; she understands the financial world, she's very urbane and sophisticated, she's very clever, I think she's perhaps cleverer than he realises, and he absolutely can't see straight for love just now. So we will see whether he has grown up.

RUPERT

I had misgivings about marrying again, but I did the decent thing – and we fought tooth and nail with a blazing row three times a day, religiously, for fifteen years . . .

I came out of my National Service in a cavalry regiment full of the ideas of an officer and a gentleman. I had a brief affair with one lady who was my first girlfriend, which didn't work out at all, and in her company I met the lady who was to become my first wife.

I was very naive, I was 21 at the time. I had a lovely house in Knightsbridge, and she made a great tilt at me, and it never occurred to me I was being conned.

She turned out to be an absolutely prolific and pathological liar. She made herself out to be something that she wasn't, and she told me a lot of things about herself which I could easily have checked, but of course I didn't. Individually, they didn't really amount to anything other than great white lies, but they put her in a category which she wasn't.

When we were in the heady romance of our first meeting she suddenly announced she was pregnant, and I was absolutely as green as they come, so I said, 'Good heavens,' and that very day we informed our respective families we were getting married. I remember my mother saying, 'This is a bit sudden, darling, wouldn't you like to wait a bit?' and I said, 'No, we've made up our minds.' An advertisement appeared in *The Times* shortly afterwards.

And gradually, after we were married, all these untruths came to light and I found I was with a rather grasping lady who then proceeded to spend all my money; I had made another great mistake of opening a joint account, and one day a very innocent cheque of mine bounced when I thought I had several thousand pounds in my account, so that didn't help.

She started drinking heavily: I would arrive home and find she'd been knocking back gins all afternoon, and in the middle of the arrival of the second child I discovered she was having an affair with three of my friends, and those three eventually disappeared from my circle of friends.

I don't remember that marriage with any affection at all, I mean I find her, still, an aggressive, deceitful, dishonest woman, still trotting out untruths left, right and centre.

I had a very upright upbringing and do you know divorce never occurred to me until I was complaining to a friend that I was very unhappy, and he said, 'Well, if you feel like that why don't you leave her . . . ?' That was a revelation to me, and I thought about it for forty-eight hours, and then I did precisely that.

I wouldn't say during that period I was tortured with inner torment, but when we split up it upset me a lot, and I kept on thinking I was doing the wrong thing. I went back to her two or three times and none of those occasions lasted more than a few days. After I left she withheld the children from me and that was agonising, because I was very fond of the children.

I had a brief affair with a beautiful actress who was the third girlfriend I'd ever had, and, on the rebound from breaking up with her, I met the person who was to become my second wife.

Number two was from a similar background to me, which I felt was in its favour, and we had a quite spirited sexual relationship.

I was in the throes of qualifying as a chartered accountant at the time and she was wonderful, she helped me through a period when I was earning virtually no money at all, plus my worldly belongings had disappeared with the first marriage.

When my divorce came through from number one, I had misgivings about marrying again, but I was under pressure from Amanda and her family, so I did the decent thing – and we fought tooth and nail with a blazing row three times a day, religiously, for fifteen years.

I eventually started to feel very unhappy and I began having affairs, and so did she. And again one of my friends was involved, my oldest and closest friend became involved with her – and so my circle of friends was diminishing rapidly with the activities of my first two wives.

Although I don't hold myself up as a paragon of virtue, I have one thing which I've stuck to all my life, I've never had an affair with a married woman, and I don't respect people who do.

And then suddenly Sue appeared on the scene and
pletely captivated by her, and within a week of meeting we
together and we became passionately fond of each other.

Some of the time I used to go over to the States on business,
what I didn't know was that two former lovers were hovering arou
feeling heartbroken that I'd come on the scene. And when our
relationship hit a slight wobbly, I said right, let's get married, so we
fixed a date.

We had the reception at the Ritz in London and went off to this sumptuous hotel on Lake Como, and the moment we got back the marriage was a constant problem.

She became distracted and offhand, and when I confronted her with it, she said, 'You're talking absolute rubbish . . .'

So, in a fit of great pique, when I knew she was meeting her sister in my flat, I rigged up a recording machine and pretended to go for a newspaper at the corner shop, left the machine on to see what these two would chatter away about, and, when I played it back, there it all was, she was having an affair.

I was absolutely brokenhearted and stunned, and I woke her up and played it back to her, and I said, 'I want you to get dressed, and get out.'

Strangely, it was as if somebody had just turned out the light, because that was twelve years ago and I have only had two very brief affairs in that time.

I was utterly devastated when wife number three left and the first person to rush to my aid was wife number two who became a stalwart friend, and I lodged with her because I was at that point nearly bankrupt.

And I have lodged here ever since, talking daily about moving out, but I haven't actually got it together yet, and all our friends and family remark on how Amanda and I don't fight and argue as we used to.

TERRY

I'll never forget, one afternoon, we were in bed, she said, 'Where are we going, Tel?' I said, 'In ten minutes we'll be down the pub.' She said, 'No, in life . . .' And then we had to have this long heart-to-heart, her idea, you see, they formulate their own ideas . . .

It wasn't love at first sight, she was just a tasty bird, and I was going out with another one at the time. Things never ran smoothly.

When she was 21 we got engaged and came within six weeks of getting married, the invitations had been printed, and that's as far as we got . . . very wisely we called it off, because there is no way that would have lasted ten minutes at that age.

It was just that I was a young lad on the tonk, I was enjoying life. I would be out doing my own thing, I'd be going out with the lads. I had other women, which was important to me at the time, but she was probably the most beautiful of the ladies, so I kept going back to her, and I went with her on and off. I didn't see her for two years, went out for six months, didn't see her for six months, and eventually we decided to get married, because it was more or less the thing to do rather than a huge new love affair. The excitement of love and holding hands, all the things you get when you're with your new girl, it only lasts a few months, doesn't it?

I do remember, the proposal, she said to me, 'Are you ever going to get married?' and I said, 'Well, I don't know that anybody would have me,' and she said, 'I would,' and that was basically it.

So we got married. I was 30 and she was 27.

It was another step in life, it was a big one, but I wouldn't say that I was overexcited. We got married in a registry office – I refused on my own religious grounds to get married in a church, and we had a lovely reception in an old Saxon mill for just the old relatives, and then we drove from there to where we had the main reception in the evening. On the way down, we had such a monster row that she threw the ring out of the car, and we'd literally been married for four hours. But we found the ring, and she put it back on, and we then had a great couple of years, they really were great.

Then the eldest son came along, and it started to become row after row. There was no theme to the rows, you suddenly realise you're rowing about everything. She would find fault with everything I did, and I would find fault with what she did. It was the standard, bickering-type things, say she was driving, quite without thinking, you say, 'You're going too slow,' and that can be taken as a monstrous criticism and start a row.

Then she got pregnant again. I cannot stand fat, that's something I absolutely detest, and I don't really like the shape of pregnant women, and during her pregnancy she became incredibly randy, so she was dying for sex. And I told her she was totally and utterly physically unattractive, which I can remember saying, and I now regret. But she was pregnant in the summer of 1976, remember how hot it was then? And I can remember not bonking her because I just didn't fancy this great big lump. I didn't realise at the time that I was being hurtful, but that is hurtful, isn't it?

She left home two or three times. But never for more than a full night, and she'd tell me exactly where she'd gone. It became silly: I'll never forget one time she said, 'I'm going,' and I said, 'Well, hang on,' and I went out and filled the car with petrol, pumped up the tyres, and reversed up the drive so she could put her bag in.

She tells me that I'm a Peter Pan-type person, and to a degree that's true, because I haven't really grown up, I suppose, but *she* changed. Before we were married she was very much one of the group, and we did have some hilarious nights out in groups, you know, all of us, but she wanted a more homely life, and her idea of a social event became either to go out to a dinner party or to invite people in, and that's never been my way of socialising.

The thing we always clashed on was the social life: her choice of friends always varied very much from mine, she liked dinner parties with her friends, who were lawyers and accountants; they were all very pleasant, but they weren't the Jack-the-lads I suppose you could call my friends.

Pubs are very important to me, the group social life. Where we were living there was a superb country pub, it really was hilarious, the landlord should have been on television years ago. And I'd say, 'I'm just going down the pub . . .' and she wouldn't go. It was quite male, well, about 95 per cent men, and it was fairly coarse, I suppose, but it was all good fun. And when skirts did come in, of course they loved it. But this all meant row after row, every time I was going down the pub: 'Why don't we go out somewhere nice?' and I'd say, 'It is a nice pub.' So I would go without her in the end.

I didn't like staying in in the evenings, I still don't, I find it quite difficult just sitting around. And male companionship is very important, always has been, I'm not a poof, but I enjoy male company.

Some nights you'd say, 'I'm just going out for a drink with the lads,' and you'd end up in mixed company, purely by circumstance . . . but I liken life to playing rugby, a good wing-forward is a good opportunist, and if the ball comes your way you take it.

Women, as you know, are different from us, and they lay it on a plate. Of course I was playing away very soon. It was exceedingly easy, and everybody was at it, I know all my friends who were 'happily' married were at it. I did have one woman who I went out with for about four or five years on the side.

A certain amount of boasting went on – male ego, isn't it? Chaps in their 50s: 'Cor, I had a nice little 25 year old last night,' it is great to talk about in the pub. But boasting wasn't the prime motivation, the prime motivation was down there hanging between your legs.

I've never understood why I needed these women, and I don't even attempt to. I did what I wanted to do. I used to call in unannounced to see this first semi-permanent girlfriend. I'd be driving along thinking: Why am I doing this, but you'd carry on, and you'd get there and have a few hours of pure blatant sex, which was very much man-sided. Women are mad, they really are, and I go a lot on the old saying that the harder you treat them the more they like you, it really is very true, especially in the case of mistresses. And I would sometimes drive along to this bird, and be totally rude to her, spend an hour in the bed having good sex, and then just drive home, and feel quite happy. I wouldn't see her more than twice a month, something like that.

You feel good, you find yourself smiling, and people would say, 'Cor, you're looking well, Tel, you're looking happy,' and it's the better you're doing on the sex side, the more buoyant you are in the rest of your life.

My wife knew. Towards the end, she said something along the

lines of, 'You're an idiot, I've known all the time what was going on . . .'

My ex-wife would tell you that I've got a problem – a standard woman's answer to a lot of emotional things is to say that you've got a problem, but I don't think I have.

Well, it became awful at home, we were rowing all the time, and in the end I just found another girlfriend, and I went off and lived with her. But I was fair, I did actually say to this other woman that I was not leaving home for her, she was just a catalyst.

I needed the catalyst. We'd talked about divorce so many times: but the conversation would always degenerate into a row: 'I hate your fucking guts,' and 'Why don't you leave home?' 'If you don't go, I will,' and, 'You can have the fucking children . . .' and this would happen almost on a weekly basis.

Well, I stayed with this woman for a while, and I set off on a new life, which wasn't that easy because I was tracked by my ex-wife, she would phone me everywhere, I think she was terribly hurt.

But I then met a lovely lady about a year after I got separated, and I think the best love affair of my life then occurred. But that fell to bits because she put the pressure on me to get married, and that was not my scene at all.

She was 31, 32, and she had reached that point where she wanted children. And I would say no way did I want children, but they try to bend you, 'Well, we'll talk about that later . . .'

I'd had a vasectomy, so I knew she couldn't do anything devious, but she did something which really made me think she was serious, she went out and got all the gen on a vasectomy reversal.

That changed my way of thinking. I had no intention of getting married to her, and marriage was basically ruling her life. I'll never forget, one afternoon, we were in bed, she said, 'Where are we going, Tel?' I said, 'In ten minutes we'll be down the pub.' She said, 'No, in life . . .' And then we had to have this long heart-to-heart, her idea, you see, they formulate their own ideas. She lived up in the Midlands, and said she was going to move down here, and I thought: This is exactly what I don't want. I need my freedom.

It was a vitriolic end, because she couldn't understand why I didn't want to get married. She then accused me of being unfaithful to her, which, in fact, believe it or not, I never was for eight months; but she had seen letters from previous girlfriends, and of course she resurrected all those into her mind as being current affairs. Why she nosed around I don't know, it always does no good, that.

I've got lots of letters, I have a box in the basement full of letters, but I do write a lot of letters, so if you write a lot you get a lot of replies, don't you?

I read once about how people write best when they're highly emotionally involved, and I wrote a letter to some bird which I wish I could get back and show you, it was the best I've ever written. It likened our love to an oak tree growing in a forest, how it outgrew the ferns, and the other trees and everything, but we had a row, and I said, 'I am the axeman, I've come to destroy our love, and it's only you, the strong oak tree, that will overcome me, the axeman . . .' I can't remember it all, it was two or three pages of superb romantic claptrap, but it was very readable, and that's me, I am a romantic.

And of course with each new affair you have more romance, which is what I think I've got started in France. I've just met a new girl in Paris, and it's wonderful. But this little girl, she's 29, she has already admitted to me that she is looking to find somebody to marry, although that hasn't put me off yet because the new romance is there, the new excitement of everything.

I've got two girlfriends on the go at the moment, it's awful, it really is, because both birds have told me they've got attached. I'm into younger women, I will be honest there, and one of them, she's too old, she's approaching my age, which is 48. I'm not really interested in her at all, but she's very lovey-dovey, phones me up, telling me, 'I'm missing you,' the sort of crap I don't want to hear, really.

But what they say about older women being better lovers is unbelievably true. God, this one I've got now – take you apart. Unbelievable. It's amazing too what middle-aged women spend on underwear, lingerie, all these things.

She married very young, and she hadn't been getting much from her husband, and they've been divorced now for three or four years, and what she's doing, like so many 40 year olds, she's making up for what she's missed in the years prior. And she really is something, I can't keep up, I tell her she needs a younger man. It does you good, though, because it keeps you going, while the excitement's still there.

For me, the absolutely ideal age is 30, 31, they've outgrown their immaturity, and they've not become old and physically floppy, because that's very important, I get put off by the flabbiness of older women.

I suppose my day of reckoning could come if I was to become ill, that's my biggest fear. When you live my sort of life you could end up ill with no women to come and visit you, because you could be in between times.

As for my wife, to say we're friends now is not the truth, basically we're just two people who didn't see eye to eye. We still don't. I went out with her last Sunday to watch my son play rugby, and she's totally intolerant to almost everything I do now, so I sit and say nothing. She doesn't see anything my way, she just sees down her own blind alley.

I don't feel any animosity towards her; I do feel sad at times because we were married fourteen years, it's a large chunk of your life.

But I would never change that, because I would never change the children, they're my pride and joy, I'd do anything for them, I really would. And I'm sure that my children are pretty well balanced.

I think she might be in love herself, although I don't ask what she's doing; but she's a very responsible lady, she wouldn't put any fellas in front of the children or do anything silly.

I'm sure that, had we not had the children, we would have got divorced after a relatively short time. We were married just over two years before she got pregnant, and those were the two romantic years.

JULIA

If he could have been forgiving we might have had a perfectly agreeable old age when all the fires had gone out, and . . . all's quiet on the Y-fronts, but I'm 60 now, and I think we would have had to wait a long time . . .

He had fallen in love with a girl who went off and married somebody else. He told me all about his disastrous arrangement with this girl: there was only second best for him, there would never be anybody else like her, etc. One night we went out to dinner and he said things had got better for him since he had known me, and I said, 'Well, there you are, you see, you should marry me,' it was a joke. However, a month later he said he had thought over carefully what I had said upon that occasion, and he thought it would be a good idea. I said, 'Oh no, no, I was joking really.' And he was devastated, he said, 'There, it's all happening again, I knew that if I trusted anybody . . .' And of course I went down like a sack of potatoes at this, which was very foolish.

I realised I had made a serious error of judgement; however, I wasn't brave enough to break it off.

We went to Naples on honeymoon and it rained a great deal, and I discovered we had even less in common than I had thought. Sex was hopeless too, but in those days nobody said it should be better, you didn't really talk about it.

We moved back into his flat and his life, and I was sort of . . . there. There was a large portrait of Palmerston in the sitting-room and everything was covered in maroon. I wanted to set about redecorating and making it look a bit brighter, but he didn't like change. In fact, he continued his life as he had run it before, there were very few concessions to marriage. He played tennis at Hurlingham at week-ends, and he went to his club for oysters at lunchtime, and when he came home he expected his dinner on the table.

We had a fierce row about something on one occasion and I picked up a glass and threw it at the fireplace, where it smashed into a million pieces. And he stood up, deeply shocked, and he said, 'Oh my God, now you're going to start breaking the place up . . .' And I laughed, because my fury had dissipated, but every time I became overheated about something he would immediately look terrified and say, 'Please don't start breaking things,' I mean, that went on for all the years I was married to him, which was frightfully irritating.

He started in politics and fought several elections and by-elections, and kept on coming second, which made him very bitter.

And then he got one, the most unexpected of them all. We were going down to the Selection Committee, and we knew somebody else was going to get it. I was wearing a brown Chanel suit, with a cream-coloured silk shirt and a pretty orange hat, I thought I looked pretty good. And he said, 'You're not going to wear that, are you?' And I said, 'Yes, I am.' And he said, 'Could you for once take me into account, this is a Conservative constituency, you're not a Liberal, why are you wearing orange?'

And I said, 'I look terrible in blue and you're not going to get it, why don't I just wear what I want to wear, for once? Why don't we all do what we want to do, for once? Why don't you give a speech about what you really feel, not just bore on about what you think they want to hear . . .' and we had a big row in the car going down.

Anyway, he made a marvellous speech, and he got the seat; nobody was more surprised than Charles, or indeed the man who was supposed to get it.

I suppose politics and things took up a lot of time, and we moved to Westminster after he became a Member of Parliament, and had a cottage in the constituency, and I had two little girls, so life was busy.

What happened then was a *coup de foudre*. I fell totally, irresponsibly, irrepressibly, unbelievably in love with a Spanish diplomat. Love. Romance. Lust. And sex, of course, which was a discovery. Everything! Sorry to say, absolutely everything. He was an enormously dynamic man, he taught me a tremendous amount about music, pictures, art and artists and places, and we shared an enormous number of things together.

I tried very hard to contain it, it was terrible really to be struck in this way, to be so hopelessly in love was dreadful, I felt such a fool, but in another way it was glorious.

But I knew that it couldn't possibly work, I knew I couldn't leave my children. I went away for a bit, and I was followed there by the Spaniard who begged me to go with him. And then Charles came over and said, 'Will you come back?' in an unemotional, English way, and he brought pictures of the children, and I said, 'Yes, of course, I will,' and I went back and started again.

Charles was terribly sad, he couldn't understand why such a thing had happened. I felt terribly sorry for him, he looked so much like he was when I first saw him, destroyed, and I had done it.

And so we started again, and tried very hard. The trouble was that he could not forgive, and it cropped up in a thousand little ways; if anybody talked about relying on people, or trust, he'd always say, 'Well, you can't really trust anybody . . .' and give me a look.

He sent me to a psychiatrist, because I suppose he thought, not unreasonably from his point of view, that there must be something dreadfully wrong with me because I wanted to leave him.

We had a number of things in common; if he could have been forgiving we might have had a perfectly agreeable old age when all the fires had gone out, and, that wonderful remark of John Gielgud's, all's quiet on the Y-fronts, but I'm 60 now, and I think we would have had to wait a long time. I probably would have taken up drink and lovers and good work.

VIRGINIA

I regret terribly that we ever got divorced, and I still think what a shame it is we are not going into old age together, because we would have been great looking after each other . . .

We got married in 1952.

I was working on the *Daily Express*, and I was scheduled to interview him, he was a test pilot. I looked him up in the cuttings, and they'd got a photograph of him, and I thought: What a lovely-looking bloke.

So when I went down to the aerodrome to meet him I was excited, because I thought: This man sounds so nice, strong and brave. I was 22, I was ready to fall in love, I think that's got a lot to do with it, timing. And it was a bit romantic for him too, he was impressed by the fact that I was already a name, and here was this very slim, not bad-looking reporter from the *Daily Express*, so it had potential, didn't it?

I got down there, he was a lodger in the Club House at the aerodrome, and he came to the door, and I remember thinking: Ooh! Nice, but he was a bit shorter than I imagined, in fact he is about my height. And he took me into the bar and we talked, and I sent him a copy of the piece when it came out. And he wrote back and said, 'Will you come down and see me here?' He wanted to meet again. I remember our first date, it was quite out of character for him, because he is a fisherman's-sweater-jeans-type bloke, but he put on a blazer and flannels, and took me to the Plough at Calderly Green. He told me afterwards that he was feeling in his pockets to see which coins were milled, which were half-crowns and which were pennies, because he was worried that he wouldn't be able to afford the bill.

And then I decided I wanted to be married, I thought it was high time really, and I don't think he did, but I persuaded him pretty well. I remember one joke we had – I made him write out, 'I promise to marry Virginia Chambers' (as I was then), and I used to flash this bit of paper at him.

Anyway, I went on a fortnight's holiday to France, and I missed him, and, as soon as I got back, I said, 'Well, what about this marriage then?' and he suddenly replied, 'Well, all right then, when?' So I said, 'What about Thursday?' and that was that, it was very hasty, it was only six weeks since we had met.

I suppose we did feel then we were right for each other. Of course I know now that one chooses one's partner for completely unconscious reasons, it's to do with previous relationships, particularly in your childhood, and we were both terribly needy people; he had been orphaned at 13 and sent off to Canada, far away from anybody he knew, and my parents had divorced when I was very young, and my mother had had very little to do with us.

We were then both caught up in a kind of euphoria, it was rush, rush, rush. We rushed to Chelsea Registry Office and got a quick licence, you only needed a couple of days' notice. He gave up his lodgings, and I had to bail him out; I paid the rent he owed in order that he could leave, and he brought all his belongings to the tiny flat I shared with my sister in Knightsbridge.

He moved in while I was at work, and when I came back there was all his stuff, and it absolutely filled the bedroom, it was half comic and half horrifying. It looked like the remains of a bankrupt circus. There was his saddle from his droving days in Canada, and chaps and stetsons, and holsters and flying kit, if you can imagine, everything to do with a man of action, which was foreign to me because I had no brothers, didn't see much of my father, had no male cousins, no uncles, and I had been to an all-girl boarding school.

He didn't know anybody in London, in fact all the guests were pals of mine, including the general manager of the *Express* who I was quite scared of, but it was nice that he came, and he unbent, and was very jolly. Everyone squeezed into the flat for the reception, and we had lots of bottles of champagne – Robbo was going absolutely wild, opening the champagne, spraying it over all the guests – and I thought: He's a bit OTT. Oh God, where is the maturity?

In fact he was a little boy lost really, how could he be otherwise, he'd had to cope on his own because of losing both his parents. But I wanted the father in him more than the child.

Directly after the reception we drove down the A4 in my funny little car, I had a car we used to call my sewing machine, because it was a Singer, it looked more like a pram, actually. We went to a country inn in the Brecon Beacons where of course I paid for the honeymoon. I've still got the bill, two nights with dinner and everything cost £17.

When we got back we rented a flat off the Fulham Road. It was a terribly lively marriage, that is the way I would put it, there were constant ups and downs and rows, but we went on hoping all the time that we could meet each other's needs. He had to go away quite a bit for his work, and we were better at separateness, actually; he used to write these wonderful letters, and I wrote lots to him, and I would then think that we'd got a good thing going.

But there was a lot of tension between us when we were together, especially if things weren't going well. He was hopeless with money, absolutely terrible; it was quite fun at first when I was paying for things, I suppose I rather liked being the person who was in charge. But we got into serious debt after the children were born, and we had to move from one house to another.

When we were really badly in debt, that was the time when he needed to spend in order to feel better: so he'd go out and buy a boat, or a car, or a brand-new cooker, or something, anything, it was just crazy. We used to have many rows over money.

I think the bits of our marriage that I resented most were when he used to go down to the local pub with his guitar, he had a lot of pals who liked making noise, you couldn't call it music; one of them, who was a right old drunk, all he used to do was bang a tin tray with a spoon.

After the children came, he would go to the pub more often, and I couldn't go because of the kids, which I quite resented. There was quite a bit of him looking at other women, some were friends of mine, and he would get them to go along to the pub with him, and I was never sure whether there was anything romantic or sexual about that. And then, gradually, he had quite a series of lovers. His attitude with affairs was: I am going to prove I am better than anybody else.

His whole life was a struggle to prove that he was better than anybody else, I think it had something to do with his height, the fact that he'd never had the approval of parents: he went deep-sea diving, he drove fast sports cars, he went out with the lifeboat people, wherever he could find a challenge that would tell him he was a real man, including sex. We were still sleeping together, I mean we still were very attracted to each other, but even while we were doing it, and I was enjoying it, I always felt: This is something for him to feel more of a man.

I tolerated these affairs, I don't know why, I suppose I felt they weren't all that important, that we had got something pretty strong. Looking at it one way, the affairs were all part of him needing approval, he needed affairs as well as what we had, nothing was enough: if you haven't had a happy childhood, you wouldn't understand, it's a sort of bottomless pit, you can never really fill that tremendous need for recognition and approval, and affairs are a way of having that. It isn't really the sex, it's having somebody wanting you, in love with you, admiring you.

He had a mistress who was married, and she decided she wanted to get a divorce, and my husband was to be cited as co-respondent. And when he told me, I just blew up: my first thought was the money situation, I felt: If he is going to have to pay damages or expenses, incur solicitors' fees, I am damned if I am going to pay for that, and we had a joint account at the time, and I insisted we separate our accounts, and he took that very hard indeed.

In the end that came to nothing, because she didn't get a divorce. We soldiered on after that, he accepted the separate accounts, although we were always having arguments about bills and everything – damn shame really about the money, he is the sort of person who should have had lots, he would have been marvellous.

Anyway, the real end came when he decided to buy a barge. He took to going to it by himself, and if we argued he'd sleep in it. And then the whole thing fell apart really. He had one girlfriend after another when he was on the barge, I think he had to show me and the girls that he could get women, and then he met a woman who was recently widowed, and it came to the point where he said he wanted a divorce.

By that time he was spending awfully little time at the house, but, at the same time, divorce seemed too much for what we were doing, which seemed to me to be just separating a bit, getting rid of the tension of always being in each other's company.

I got very depressed and sad, and I was angry too. I can remember going down to the barge when he had got a woman there: you couldn't just walk on to the barge and knock at the door, it was moored a bit out in the stream, he was always somebody who would get as far away from people as he possibly could. You had to stand on the bank and shout 'Ahoy' – whatever the name of the barge was – 'Willow', 'Ahoy, Willow' . . . And I remember doing this once because I desperately wanted to talk about the children, and it was ages before he would come to the gangway; and eventually he came up, and I shouted across, 'Can we talk, we must talk . . .' 'No, I can't now . . .' And he wouldn't talk. And I remember, I drove back from there in tears, recognising that this was the end, because he wouldn't even talk, and after a two-year separation we got a divorce by mutual consent.

It's a tragedy that should never have happened, I regret terribly that we ever got divorced, and I still think what a shame it is we are not going into old age together, because we would have been great looking after each other.

I think it helps an awful lot if you have someone on the scene who is interested in you, or you have an affair quite soon after a divorce. Of course what you do get is a hell of a lot of men you thought were friends coming along, saying, 'You must be in need of it . . .' 'I bet you miss the sex.' I was astonished, it sounds such a cliché, doesn't it, but they do come round, like bees round a honey pot with a newly unattached woman.

I can remember one man, God, he was slimy, he had been a good friend of Robbo's, he came round, said he would just like a chat for old time's sake. And he brought with him these postcard-sized pictures of women in funny poses. I don't think I had known any kinky people or come across this kind of thing, and it shocked me terribly, I suppose I thought: God, is this what I am in for now, is this what it means when you haven't got a man?

Oh, I still love him, I don't think you can live with somebody for twenty-one years and have no feelings for them, and I don't have any resentment or hate or anything – I wish he was still about.

He came for Annie's wedding, and our dealings with each other are warm, very warm, we chat on the phone and send each other cuttings that might interest or amuse, and exchange birthday presents and things; his wife is not too happy about that, and he has to be very careful not to upset her, but we don't have bitter feelings, the loving feelings are still there. I love him very much, and it would hurt me dreadfully if he were ill and I wasn't able to be there. Particularly if he was dying. I don't know whether his wife would tell me, but I would love to be able to say to her, Look, please, if Robbo is ever really ill, will you let me come and see him?

DANIEL

For a long time I felt sexually ambivalent . . .

My father left Germany at the age of 19, the sky falling in on his head. He lost his parents in Auschwitz, and I grew up with the aftermath of that – well, it was hardly an aftermath, the loss was very present to me as a kid, the realities of the gas chambers were pretty vivid.

I felt put upon. Both my mother and father called me Father, and they seemed to me like kids: 12 years old and your parents call you Father, then the possibilities of disaster are quite big. And I never trusted the world, and I still haven't really found a good reason to do so. I can never relax, I don't see why the fuck I should. I fear the human being's capacity for acting cruelly and stupidly towards other people.

We had a rather rocky start, to some degree influenced by her parents' disapproval of me; it was difficult to understand why they disapproved, because they had never met me. Then they met me and disapproved even more. I think it was because I wasn't going to be a doctor or a lawyer, and they had this idea that their daughter should be married off to only the best, and I didn't look like only the best to them. I wanted to be a writer but I was only a journalist.

The honeymoon was very beautiful, and memorable – but I always felt, and probably still do: Is this it? Is this all there is to it? There's got to be more to it. I wanted everything to be terribly important, tinged with significance, tinged with melodrama, I wanted every night to be gala night, very intense conversations and very powerful, meaningful sex.

And what I got was ordinary life. I can remember a feeling, which I tried very hard to suppress: This is just ordinary life, all I am doing is walking down a hotel corridor, I am having breakfast with my wife in a hotel, and it's very nice – but I wanted more than just very nice.

I felt sexually very indecisive. I felt that sexual exclusivity was a hard burden for me to bear, and I had a tendency if not towards promiscuity, at least alternatives. For a long time I felt sexually ambivalent, and I think total commitment to one person and what that would mean in terms of having to forswear all the other parts of the spectrum I felt made up my sexual life was terrifying, and it manifested itself in various attempts to be unfaithful.

Most of my attempts to be unfaithful were unsuccessful; when it came down to it, I was quite timid, and I was not very charming.

The first person I was actually unfaithful with was a prostitute. That was frighteningly unsatisfying.

And I explored my bisexuality – thank God AIDS wasn't around then.

I managed to find someone through the columns of *Time Out*. I only saw him twice. I remember finding it sexually very gratifying, and in every other way wanting to run away from this as quickly as possible. I wanted the guy for sexual gratification and that was it, I didn't want anything else to do with him. It was very callous.

I told Cath, I was incredibly open about my inclinations, and I kept on trying to persuade her that this was perfectly natural and it posed no threat to our marriage, and she just had to accept that. And clearly, understandably, that was not how she saw things, and over a period of time she became increasingly distant.

When you're on that sort of kick, the only way you can go is more and more of the same, and, more bizarre, I was in a state of constant need for excitement, it's a bit like alcoholism, it is an addiction.

I tried to persuade Cath to become interested in women, she tried very hard to play a role that I had decided was going to be a turn-on for me, and she met a girl at a Joan Armatrading concert, and brought her to our home, and I joined them.

I felt: Is this all? So this is all. It was profoundly unsatisfying, the whole fucking thing was profoundly unsatisfying.

One thing around that time really shocked and frightened me. Catherine and I were using a Ouija board and we raised some voice that spelled out to me, 'S-T-O-P B-E-I-N-G U-N-F-A-I-T-H-

F-U-L T-O Y-O-U-R W-I-F-E.' How the hell that happened I don't know.

We continued to have a sexual relationship until she decided to pack her bags and go off with her yoga teacher.

After Catherine left I was distraught, utterly distraught. I was frightened, I felt dreadfully abandoned, I was in a terrible state. I went to see a shrink for the first time. I was very much in need of comfort, and I hated being alone, and I felt very sorry for myself – I felt incredibly sorry for myself, well, maybe I enjoyed feeling sorry for myself, I have a propensity towards self-pity. I cried a lot. I was free but I was in pain, and I wanted the pain to stop.

I visited Catherine. She had moved to a squat near Regent's Park, and I'd go over and sit on the floor, and have long conversations. I implored her to come back and eventually she did. We went for a walk on Hampstead Heath and bought some mangoes, and we got stoned, there was a lot of dope around in those days. Eating mangoes was the most orgasmic sensation, and we made love, and then she asked me to hit her, to beat her on her breasts as a way of expiation, I suppose, for leaving me.

I found that interesting, but I don't think I've ever been able to abandon myself to hurting anyone.

We got back together and Max was born the following spring.

His arrival was devastating.

Cath has the baby, and, two days later, I've never been so ill in my life. I was incapable of helping her, I was lying on a bed hallucinating about smells I had had as a kid myself.

And when he was 18 months old I packed up and left . . .

And that was it, that was the end of it. No, that wasn't the end of it, I gave her the house and she allowed me access to my son. She put aside her hurt to enable me to maintain a relationship with Max. Now we talk about Max and we worry about his schooling, and so I have a relationship with my son thanks to my wife, thanks to her big heart.

Life goes on, it's a sort of life, I suppose, I really oughtn't to complain. I have inflicted more pain than I would like to have done.

I find it hard to comprehend, and hard not to be disgusted. The picture I'm painting of myself is of such a hateful creature. I feel incredibly judged by what I've been saying, I feel like saying, Tell me I've not said that.

Help me, I'm scared . . .

KATE

Sexually speaking, we were in the Kindergarten, building our blocks and having a nice time in the sexual sandpit, but I don't think we progressed out of it . . .

We met at university in Australia. He was kind of Mr Wonderful, he had what were widely regarded as being perfect masculine attributes, he was very tall and blond and handsome and kind and athletic, and I fell in love with him.

Ashley invited me to the college house ball, that was the actual event that set it off, and I remember that ball very well. It was a starry night, very romantic, and we danced with each other all night; and that was it for us, we fell in love very quickly and romantically and ideally, and we were inseparable for the three years that followed.

And then there was no question about it, we were made for each other, we were going to get married as soon as we left university, and that is precisely what we did, we got married about two weeks after graduating.

We had a brief honeymoon, we went to the mountains by a beautiful lake, and bummed around catching fish. There was a bit too much catching fish for my liking. Ashley likes nothing more than to stand in a river with a rod in his hand for hours on end, and I thought: God, is it going to be like this, fishing, and nothing happening? I suppose I thought it was going to be more exciting, so it was a bit of a let down in a way.

The honeymoon was extended on board ship, because Ashley had a graduate apprenticeship with an engineering firm in Swansea, and we went to Britain by sea, which took six weeks, and that was pretty boring too, I have to say, but then six weeks at sea can be.

Swansea was a come down. We got settled into a flat and Ashley started his job, and suddenly life kind of stopped for me. I had had this notion that I was marrying this perfect chap and my life was going to be taken care of: I wasn't going to have to think for myself, because being his wife, having his children, looking after his house was what I was going to do. But suddenly, there you are in this flat, and your new husband has gone off to work, and the door slams and it is nine o'clock in the morning. I was desperately lonely and miserable, and missing university life, I just wondered, here I am, 21 years old and now what . . . ?

I got a job in a secondary-modern school in a fairly rough part of Swansea. And I found trying to keep discipline and control of a classroom of forty girls, not that much younger than me, pretty terrifying. And I really couldn't do it, just trying to keep order was more than I could cope with.

That sort of thing knocks you. Ashley was sympathetic, but trying to talk to him about things was always a problem, he didn't express his own feelings, he wasn't good at analysing anyone else's, and, in a way, from the moment I met him I was never able to talk with him about feelings and emotions. Ashley has always been, and is still as far as I know, a very undemonstrative and unexpressive person. Ashley was always saying, 'I love you, you love me, and that's it, nothing more to be said.' And that *was* it, and I felt at a loss from the beginning.

I never doubted his caring or feeling for me, but I missed some evidence of passion. He never expressed passion, violent feelings, anger, pleasure.

Sex was rather similar, I suppose; my feeling about sex is you only learn about your own sexuality when you are very active, very progressive, very open on the sexual front. I was really just in the kindergarten class with him sexually speaking; we were building our blocks and having a nice time in the sexual sandpit, but I don't think we progressed out of it.

When I became pregnant, Ashley was absolutely noninvolved, he didn't want to be anywhere near the hospital at the birth.

But I was sort of relieved to be pregnant: a. because it got me out of teaching at that awful school, and b. I thought: Well, we can get on with this bit, still not thinking for myself about what I wanted to do, or could do.

And then there was a new turn in Ashley's career, he was picked out to be a kind of roving salesperson for his company, and was going to be sent around to various parts of the world for the next six or seven years, which is what we did.

And so when Amy was about 18 months and I was expecting Guy, we went off to Montreal, and Guy was born there. We then had this very peripatetic period where we had about a year in Montreal, four months in Winnipeg, six months in San Francisco, four months in Washington DC which actually coincided with John Kennedy's death, and we arrived there the week he was assassinated, and went to the funeral, which was a very powerful, unforgettable experience.

This is where the change in my attitude took place – in fact, I can pinpoint it to the four months we spent in Winnipeg. It was in the middle of the winter, I couldn't go outside without three-quarters of an hour bundling up the children to get them dressed for those freezing temperatures, and I felt utterly trapped, and almost immediately I sank in a major gloom. I didn't have any friends, we had rented a house which was a nasty little box in a suburb somewhere, and the children were at that age where they were most demanding. I reached the point of watching television in the day with the children just because it kept everybody quiet, and that was when I thought: I have got to do something.

I was still only 23/24 and at a point where I had enormous energy and interest in life, and sex, and all of this was closing down, and here I was stuck in this nasty little house with no options, it seemed like that anyway. We didn't stay there long, thank God, it really was a grim place.

Also, I read a book. I read Betty Friedan's *The Feminine Mystique*, which described my predicament in such a vivid way that it seemed like the book had been written for me. I can remember reading it, avidly, with a growing excitement and pleasure, realising that my unexpressed frustration was being expressed and articulated by someone else. And that was tremendous because it gave me some glimmers of hope that there were other ways of living my life. I had no one to talk to about it, I didn't talk to Ashley about it, but that book was very influential on my thinking.

And then we got sent off to San Francisco, and we found a beautiful flat overlooking the bay on Telegraph Hill, and that was exciting, because this was 1962, and the North Beach area was filled with jazz clubs, and you had the remnants of the fifties beatnik clubs, and we went to the famous *The Hungry i*, and saw Eleanor Bron, Peter Cook, etc. And that was terribly exciting because one realised that something was going on, this was a first sign that the establishment was being got at, and that gave me a tremendous kick. I don't think Ashley was ever as questioning and anti-establishment as me, he was much more conventional and conservative – so we were beginning to diverge there.

From San Francisco we drove all the way across the southern states, through New Orleans, up through Maryland, and ended up in Washington DC, and we lived in Alexandria over the Potomac River, in a very beautiful house. And that was where I did my first bit of modelling for a woman I met there, and some pictures appeared in the *Washington Post*, which was great fun.

And then we went off to Brazil for four years, and that was really the place that opened up the whole world to me, and the possibilities of a different future.

I was absolutely amazed that, arriving in a place I had never thought about and knew nothing about, I would feel more at home and more excited than I had anywhere else. I just stepped off the aeroplane, took a whiff of Brazil, and I was away. It went through me like a shot of adrenalin: an enormous feeling of happiness, well-being, pleasure. We had a nice house in the middle of downtown São Paulo, which you might not think is heaven on earth, but in fact it was so vibrant, so full of life and activity and energy, there was a complete mêlée of races, of cultures, of people, of types. And I just loved the people, loved the music, loved the atmosphere, the heat, we had a sort of market fair in our street every Friday, and there was enormous bustle and activity. Not to say Ashley didn't like it, because he did, but he was working in an English office every day, spoke only English to English people. I got caught up in the fashion business doing modelling jobs, and in fact became really quite well known as a photographic model. And it gave me an entrée into a very interesting bunch of people, journalists, designers, photographers, artists, musicians, and I learnt to speak Portuguese quite fluently. And so I used to go off and do these jobs, and it was exciting, it was fun, it was great for my ego and confidence, and of course I was an *Inglesa* at a time in the sixties when to be English was everything in fashion, there was Mary Quant and Biba, who came out to Brazil, and I modelled for her, and Paco Rabanne and Rudi Gernreich.

And then inevitably I got caught up in an affair, which was the first sexual experience I had had outside the marriage – it was a real education.

I met an Argentinian who lived in Brazil. He was a gorgeous-looking beachboy, your typical Latin lover. Sexually I was incredibly inexperienced, and he taught me a lot of things, and it was extremely sexy.

Well, he talked all the time, and of course it was all in Portuguese which I found especially sexy. Ashley, as you've gathered, was a fairly taciturn fellow, didn't have a lot to say about anything . . . this guy talked and talked and talked right through making love, and said a lot of what I found very sexy things about me, about us. And he used words very seductively, very sexy, his use of language. And he was very physical, and very, very demanding, and, it has to be said, he was masterful. He would boss me around and say, '*Venca, venca.*' ('Come here, come here.') I thought this was wonderful. He also liked making love in front of mirrors – I think mainly to look at himself, which was a completely new experience for me. I imagine he would be ghastly to live with or to know better than I knew him.

The whole place was vibrating sex. I used to go up to Rio occasionally for weekends, and there the place was throbbing and he had a little flat on Copacabana Beach, which was just amazing.

But then with all of that very heady stuff went the deception, telling lies and making up stories as to what I was doing. I have a feeling Ashley was aware of what was going on, but he never said a word. I would come back after a night of passion on Copacabana Beach and feel pretty bad next day when I'd have to make up some story about what I'd been doing.

This all had a very deleterious effect on our sex life, which had since the birth of the children become very sporadic and lacklustre anyway. And we had become pretty estranged, we had lost any intimacy that we had had. And I was very unhappy by then, the duplicity made me feel wretched, and I began to see the marriage was not going to last, and that I had to get out of it.

When we went back to Swansea again, it was disastrous, dreadful. *It* was unchanged, and for me everything had changed, and I didn't want to be there – I wanted to be anywhere but there, I didn't want to be with Ashley, I wanted to be back in Brazil, and I wanted to work, I wanted to take charge of my own life.

And so I started to look for a job, and eventually I got one, and moved down to London, and set about finding a place to live, and schools for the kids.

It was terribly difficult working and looking after the children, and there were lots of financial worries, but I took no money for myself from Ashley, I never felt he owed me a living.

I began living a much more honest life than I'd been living before, politically, emotionally, certainly personally and professionally. For the first time I was actually making my own way, my own living. I think it was this dependence, particularly financial and emotional dependence on one person, one man, that just didn't work for me.

DEIRDRE

By then he was working at a trendy advertising agency, and he was a dapper little smartly dressed, sixties, flower-shirted young charmer, and I was a drab, harassed, overweight young housewife with two toddlers, hard up, miserable, depressed, and I'm not in the least surprised that he had an affair with his secretary . . .

We were at Cambridge together, and at the beginning of my last term of my last year, which was 1961, I met him at a party. He was there with a very good-looking, red-headed American girl, but I have to say that our eyes met across the room and something went zing, which is extraordinary, because I was short and bespectacled and absolutely nothing to look at. And he took me back to my college at the end of the party, much to the fury of the guy who brought me, to say nothing of the American girl.

I think that, as so often in my life, I picked him, and then brought an amazing energy to bear upon getting him – and to find himself the object of such intense energy and desire was very flattering for him. I have nearly always chosen my men, and, having picked the unfortunate victim, I bend my strength and my desires to getting them, and I did this with Crispin.

He was quite nice-looking, but really exceptionally charming, it was a genuine effervescence of personality, he was one of the most charming men I have ever met, which was quite unusual in 21 year olds, and without fail people were charmed by him, I certainly was, and to be swept along in the wake of this charm was just devastating.

I was greatly lacking in charm, I was very gauche and awkward, but in exchange for this charm I could make him laugh a great deal. He's one of the fairly few people in my life who found me incredibly funny, and I could reduce him to tears of laughter . . . he would beg me to stop.

Very quickly we began to see each other just about every day. He had rooms in St John's looking out over the Cam, and I would go and stand underneath his rooms and shout 'Crispin' until his head poked out of the window, and he would come down and get me. And I would then sit in his room and have tea or coffee, and we would work together, and about three weeks later we slept together, and it was the first time for both of us – despite his charm and looks, he too was still a virgin.

I am surprised in retrospect that it took us three weeks to sleep together, but it was a very major step. I had been extremely strictly brought up in terms of sexual morals, my family was extremely puritanical, indeed all sexuality and all physicality was completely taboo in our household. And I had not really expected to sleep with anybody until I was married – so the fact that I went to bed with Crispin and continued to do so signified to me that this was the man I was probably going to marry.

I had never seen a naked man before, ever, and had very little idea of what one did. I do remember at some crucial point on that night I asked, 'Are we there, have we done it?' And he said, 'If we haven't done it, we never will.' We were both so ignorant that we didn't know if penetration had actually taken place, but we just sort of concluded that it had. It seemed OK at the time, it wasn't wonderful, it wasn't earth-shaking, but it was all right.

From that moment on I did no more work and was so besotted that I actually used to walk out early from examinations in order to go and be with Crispin. Not surprisingly I got a very bad degree.

Sometime in July or August, Crispin came down to stay at my parents' house for the weekend, and naturally we slept together. And the next day my mother in changing the sheets realised what had happened, and was outraged, astonished, horrified, distressed, went pounding down to the kitchen to tell my father. I can hardly convey quite what a rigid and puritanical and sexless household this was – and it certainly hadn't for a moment entered my parents' heads that I would sleep with anybody before marriage. And my father said, and, God knows, I shall never forget these words: 'I would rather have heard that you had committed murder than that you were no longer a virgin.' And he gave me ten shillings and told me to take myself up to London. Now I don't know what they thought would happen, I don't know whether they thought I would come back at the end of the day weeping and penitent and promise to turn over a new leaf, but I went up to London and never came back. And that is how I came to have my own flat in London, and Crispin, who was a year behind me, came down from Cambridge for long weekends and stayed with me in the flat, and in January 1964 we got married.

Once my parents heard we were going to get married, that he was making an honest woman of me, they gave their approval.

In fact, leaping ahead, when we divorced, my parents took Crispin's side, since it was predictably enough their view that it is the job of the wife to hold on to her husband, and that, if the husband leaves, the wife must have done something wrong.

I must say that when we got married I still had never been to bed with anybody except Crispin, and I distinctly remember walking up the aisle towards him and thinking: Now I will never kiss any other man, and I was quite sure, and not even particularly regretful, that the next fifty, sixty years of my life were committed to this man, and the possibility of divorce did not enter my head.

The honeymoon was a weekend away with a couple of friends of ours from Cambridge, and I conceived on my wedding night – it was a mere stroke of good fortune that I hadn't conceived at any time in the previous eighteen months. So, nine months later, to Crispin's horror, we had a child. I say to his horror, because he wasn't very well paid – he was earning about eight pounds a week at the time, and the rent was four pounds a week. Fortunately, he was a very good card player, and he used to go out every week and play poker or bridge – mainly poker because you can win more, and, if he hadn't played poker and won consistently, I don't know how we would have lived.

I'm astounded that I got pregnant the second time, sex was almost nonexistent, we incredibly seldom made love, once a month, sometimes less. He said to me from the very beginning really that he didn't find me sexually attractive, that I was interesting, and he liked talking to me, and he liked the way I entertained our friends, in other words, I had good wife potential as far as looking after him and furthering his career, but sexually he was quite uninterested in me. But I always knew that. I certainly knew it before we got married.

Things started going wrong very quickly indeed, they started going wrong as soon as he knew I was pregnant. He had imagined that we would have a very social, glamorous life as young marrieds in London. He thought that we would be giving dinners and go to the theatre and parties, and the Establishment, which was the trendy nightclub of the time; he hadn't reckoned with being dragged down by nappies and broken nights – and poverty above all. I don't know that he exactly blamed me, it's just that it wasn't what he had envisaged.

I knew I wasn't happy, and yet we were very close. For example, I was suddenly taken ill when I was pregnant with the second child, and I was rushed into hospital where I very nearly died. And Crispin would come and sit with me in the morning before going to work and in the evenings when he got back from work, and although already things were very bad between us, he would pour strength into me just by being there. And, after an hour or so of him there, I would feel better and I could sit up and think of eating, and he would be absolutely drained. Now that seems to me to be a very married thing to happen between people.

But at the same time he was already having an affair.

Within a year of our being married he started an affair with an extremely good-looking and vivacious woman whose husband was a BBC producer who was away in Africa researching a programme, and indeed she conceived a child by him, and so he had to go through all the business of the abortion.

When he told me of this first affair I was devastated, because, just as I'd believed I was married for ever, I also believed that we would be faithful together – the naivety seems criminal in retrospect.

By then he was working at a trendy advertising agency, and he was a dapper little smartly dressed, sixties, flower-shirted young charmer, and I was a drab, harassed, overweight young housewife with two toddlers, hard up, miserable, depressed, and I'm not in the least surprised that he had an affair with his secretary.

We'd been having a lot of rows, and one morning he said, 'I'm not going to go to work today, I have to talk to you,' and he rang up the office and said he wouldn't be coming in. He took me for a walk on Hampstead Heath, which was near where we lived, and he said, 'I've fallen in love with Judy' – I knew who Judy was – 'and I want to leave you and live with her.' I remember, I lay down on the ground on Hampstead Heath, I couldn't cry, I couldn't even think of anything to say, and he just stood there. I realised then that he was already quite emotionally detached from me, because, if he had any real feeling or sympathy for me, he could not have failed to take me in his arms. He just stood and waited until I'd pulled myself together, and after about ten minutes I got up and we walked on.

And a few weeks after that he left. We had been married less than four years and we had two children . . .

Sitting here now I am overwhelmingly grateful that the marriage broke up that fast, because, had we stuck it out for ten years, I would have been disqualified by absence from the working scene, and by low self-esteem and all kinds of other things from ever working other than as a secretary.

But it wouldn't have gone on for ever, because he would have had one mistress after another, and I wouldn't have put up with that indefinitely – if he hadn't left me, I dare say I would have kicked him out eventually. If I hadn't, he would have cramped me out of all recognition, I would have become bitter and vicious and spiteful and manipulative and terribly unhappy, I think I would have punished life for having bound me up with this man.

Also, it's quite clear to me that he is totally not husband material. He follows the same pattern every time. He marries, finds a mistress, dumps the wife, marries the mistress, finds a mistress, dumps the wife, and he's done it five times now.

And yet his leaving me was incredibly difficult. I had projected that marriage would last until I died, and unwinding that expectation I found unbelievably painful. This was separate from what I felt for Crispin: we had had a lot of rows, I knew that he was vain and shallow and unreliable and flirtatious, I knew that he wasn't nearly as clever as me, but I had committed my life to him and we had these two children, and unpicking that commitment was astonishingly difficult. I found that the state of being a single woman again was very exposed and very painful. I felt as though I had been living under one of those great glass cheese dishes, and from inside it I could see the world and I could see everything that was happening, but suddenly somebody had lifted the lid off, and I was exposed to cold winds and bad smells, all the reality.

The reality was that it was very difficult having a full-time job and coping with two toddlers who were very demanding. I had a nanny, but only during the day, and I found the sheer practicalities of trying to keep the family going and pay for them very very hard. Crispin said when he left, 'Don't ever ask me for money because I won't give you a penny . . .' And he never did.

It was incredibly difficult telling my parents and my friends that Crispin had left me. I was the first of my contemporaries to divorce, I can't remember anybody else divorcing for at least five years. And people were either quite shocked, or, in the case of the married men, and some of the single men too, I suddenly became a 'safe fuck', and from having been extremely innocent and inexperienced and virginal I did in the next few years go to bed with a very large number of men, not always because I wanted to.

I went to bed with men because they gave me lifts home from parties, I went to bed with men because they asked me. One did in the sixties, unless you had a very good reason not to, and after all I was on the pill, I had my own double bed, and I hadn't got a husband. Nevertheless, I think that I remained sexually extremely immature and ignorant until I was in my early 30s when I had an affair with a very practised lover who was in fact the father of my third child, and who was very good for me in all kinds of ways.

But I had a very tough time.

The first and most overwhelming reason is that I was desperately poor. I was bringing up two children, and from 1972 three children, with no support from my ex-husband, no support from my parents, who bitterly disapproved of the divorce, and passionately disapproved of my becoming pregnant without being married, I mean that shocked them just as much as the initial loss of virginity had shocked them. So I had no financial support and not much moral support either. I was working, trying to run a household, trying to pay a mortgage, and I was a very bad mother, I got angry with them, I neglected them emotionally – and that is incomparably the biggest regret of my life. They are grown up into excellent people, they are devoted to each other, they are devoted to me, we're very close, but it's remarkable that they came through it, because the affect of the divorce upon them, although they were so small, was harrowing. And Crispin was a very indifferent father. He didn't come and see them very often, even when he said he was coming he often cancelled, he was always much more preoccupied with the latest young wife or mistress. I suppose he saw them five or six times a year, usually for a Sunday afternoon.

The unhappy period used to have temporary remissions – when I fell in love with somebody. I wanted to fall in love, I quite badly wanted to get married again. And yet, when an eminently suitable friend of Crispin's told me he had been in love with me throughout our marriage – and he was a dear man, a sweet man, he would have done me ideally in many ways, if I had simply wanted marriage I could not have found a more convenient man, well paid, good family, mad about me, sweet with the children . . . but I didn't love him. I have spent my adult life passionately in pursuit of love, and I feel guilty about that because I think I should have done what a lot of divorced women do, and that is to turn their emotional and sensual needs towards their children.

Now anybody who pursues love as passionately as I did obviously finds it a lot, and I have had a number of very good and very happy and very fulfilling relationships, one of which lasted for four years with a man who lived with me, although at the last minute we didn't actually get married. The affair with James's father was glorious, quite astonishingly ecstatic, and among other things I made a great many male friends with whom I have never been to bed, but of whom I am extremely fond. I think that my life as a single woman has been incomparably richer and more detailed and more maturing than if I had stayed a wife.

On the other hand, the fact that I did marry and had children saved me from a lot of the angst of my contemporaries who, if they hadn't married, were getting very frantic about having children by the time they were in their mid-30s. I didn't have that. I'm extremely glad that I had children so young, because I think it is gruellingly hard work, and I don't envy anybody who starts on it in their late-30s.

I hardly ever think of that marriage. Years go by without seeing my ex-husband. The last time I saw him was at the christening of our two younger grandchildren, and Crispin was there with wife number five. It was about eight years since I had last seen him, and I didn't know how I would react to his being there, and when he came over to speak to me I ignored him, I just wouldn't look at him. The reason for my anger is not at what he did to me, I think my anger was at the way he treated the children who did go on loving him and needing him and whom he kicked in the teeth time and time again . . .

I think we should have broken up that first summer after we met. One weekend my parents were away, and of course Crispin came over to stay, in spite of my having sworn blind that he wouldn't. And we had a terrific row. I've no idea now what it was about, but he stormed out, and for a week or so I was frightfully unhappy and cried a lot. And I then began to reconcile myself to the fact that he had gone. After about ten days or so, he walked up the garden path, and he had been to see his sister who had said, 'She's a decent girl, you must stick with her,' and he had done what his sister said. And even at that moment I knew that I was already getting over him, and there was even a part of me that regretted he had come back. We should have broken up that summer.

I also remember a moment when we had been married about two years, and we were on holiday in Scotland. We had had a tremendous row one evening and I said something like, 'Well, if it's as bad as that you can always divorce me.' And I knew then that the word had been uttered, and that I shouldn't have said it, because the moment you speak the word you make it a possibility. I knew that that was the beginning of the end, and I took the boat and rowed out into the middle of the loch. It was getting dark, and I was cold, and I felt an awful fool, but I rowed about in circles while Crispin walked up and down the beach swinging a lantern and calling me. I wanted him to be worried, I wanted him to think I had drowned.

It was fifteen or sixteen months later that he actually left me, but that was the moment at which it became possible.

KATHLEEN

I now know high-heels are not something anyone should wear in Venice . . . The first day of our honeymoon he insisted on marching ahead, and he began shouting at me for not being able to keep up with him, and eventually he was so far ahead I got lost, and I didn't know how to get back to the hotel, and I was wandering around for hours . . .

I met him at a dance, he was rather outrageously dressed, flamboyant would be how I would describe his appearance and demeanour, I thought he was the most horrible, arrogant man I had ever met, and he was so unusual and such a strange mixture that it was compelling. He was ten years older than me, he was a history professor, a very knowledgeable, worldly type.

We ran into each other for over two years at dinner parties before anything ever happened, we would try to top each other being entertaining and stealing the stage.

And then I had really bad glandular fever for six months and he was one of the few friends that really bothered to correspond, and he sent me amusing letters and anecdotes about things that were happening, and one note which said, 'As soon as you are well get in touch,' and the weekend I got back he invited me down to his parents' house in the country, and that's when things started.

He liked the fact that I was American, he always made rude remarks about English girls, about how stupid they were, how uneducated and unambitious, and he couldn't talk to them. And I loved the idea of going out with an Englishman – I'm afraid a lot of American girls find Englishmen very attractive.

Well, he proposed within six months, and I contacted my parents and they came over from America, and we had dinner. And he kind of backed away from the whole situation, so much so that he never mentioned marriage or anything at dinner. My parents were looking at me, like: Why have we come all this way to meet this guy . . . ? I challenged him immediately my parents left, and he said, 'I never asked you ,' he denied it entirely. So we had a huge row, and I told him to go to hell, and a few weeks later he came crawling back and said maybe marriage wasn't such a bad idea . . .

He then properly asked me to marry him, and I was the one saying, 'I am not so sure,' and then eventually I said yes.

And my parents at that exact moment said, 'Darling, don't do it.' My father said, 'There is not enough room in his heart for you, because it is all filled with himself.'

I was upset by that, I knew best, they didn't know him, they didn't understand him the way I did; but every member of my family tried to talk me out of it from the moment I announced my engagement.

I myself had a few little niggling doubts, the main one was about children, something I could never get him to talk about. The week before the wedding I made him come to the West End and have lunch with me, and I said, 'Well, what do you think about children?' and he said, 'Not for five or six years,' and I said, 'But you do want them, don't you?' And he said, reluctantly, yes, and that was our entire conversation, which made me a little nervous, but I thought: It's probably going to be OK, hope for the best . . .

The honeymoon was not so good. I'd never been to Venice, he'd been there a hundred times before, Italian architecture is his passion, but I think he was rather irritated at having another person along. I had bought a wonderful trousseau, fantastic daytime outfits and high-heels, although I now know high-heels are not something anyone should wear in Venice . . . Our first day out he insisted on marching ahead, and he began shouting at me for not being able to keep up with him, and eventually he was so far ahead I got lost, and I didn't know how to get back to the hotel, and I was wandering around for hours. Somehow I got back, but it was very disappointing, the first day of your honeymoon to have your husband take off. When we went out to dinner he was distant, I think it had hit him that he had got married, and he was trying to run away from it, literally! To be honest, I was really glad to get back to London five days later.

We moved into his house, and he was most reluctant to get rid of his lodgers: he is so mean, he got just £10 a week from these people, and he is so rich it is unbelievable; to his sadness I got rid of the lodgers and then I went out and found us a new house.

He always pretended he was poor, and never, the whole time we were married, did I have an allowance, I had to support myself entirely. But worse than that I used my savings for the five or six years of my marriage, and I was too ashamed to tell my parents that the money they gave me for wedding presents I used as living expenses.

What can you say? Love is blind, and he had a very forceful personality. I knew it was wrong but I didn't know what to do about it.

And three years in I had an undiagnosed illness, and I went into hospital for six weeks; it was complete inertia, I couldn't move, I couldn't do anything, and of course they asked, 'Do you have a happy marriage?' and I'd say, 'Of course I do.' What are you going to say, No, I secretly hate my husband and this is why my body has stopped functioning?

I couldn't admit how unhappy I was because everyone had told me not to do it, and, being a Catholic, I take really seriously the idea that marriage is for ever, and once together never asunder, and all that. I thought: I've been married in church and I just have to keep working at it, and the nicer I am to him and the more I do for him, the more he is going to love me.

I come from a large family, and no one in my whole sphere of extended family is divorced, but my parents who are very strict Catholics were saying to me divorce him, divorce him, he's awful.

Part of our whole problem had been that he didn't want to have children and I very much wanted them. I finally got him to say OK, and of course I got pregnant within two minutes. I was so happy, I set up a candlelit dinner: 'Darling, I have the most wonderful news, I am pregnant,' and, silence – worse than silence – and that kind of reaction is the last thing anyone wants.

But I thought: I have done this thing, I must go through with it. We got closer to the baby arriving, and he wouldn't let me buy any baby clothes, or do anything to the house to make preparation for this child, it was as if by ignoring it it would go away. We had a very beautiful, very sophisticated London town house, all velvet and damask and so on, but no room for children, and I would say, 'Can we put a little play-room here?' 'No, we are not going to do it until the baby comes.' And then, finally, I was seven months pregnant and I felt a bit funny and called the doctor, and he said come in immediately, and Spencer wouldn't take me there, so one of the builders who was in the house drove me there, and waited for me.

It was not good news, there was something wrong and I had to be admitted to hospital immediately. The baby was born with something terribly wrong with it, we got one who was so severely handicapped that they did what they do in those circumstances, they just don't resuscitate them. Spencer wouldn't come to see me in the hospital. This is a moment when you need a husband that wants a child, this is not a moment when you need someone that wants to run away. Well, my twin sister, God bless her, came over from America, and she held my hand through the whole thing and she was wonderful. Spencer found it all so traumatic, he said, 'I have to get away, I just can't stand it, I know you will understand . . .' and he went to Paris with a girlfriend for four days and left me in the hospital with my twin. And I believed him, I believed that he was suffering too, and this was his way of dealing with it. And I said, 'Yes, do go and I will be here when you come back,' and so he vanished.

Martha, my twin, then said, 'You must leave him, he is evil,' but she knew something I didn't know – which is that, while she was staying in my house while I was in hospital, he had crawled into her bed.

I then got angry, and I went to Charles Jaw, the eye-gouger lawyer of London. I figured: I can't hurt this guy through his heart, because he hasn't got one, but I can hurt him through his pockets, it's the only thing that hurts him. I thought: OK, if he wants a divorce he can get one. Jaw can be pretty aggressive but is an extremely good divorce lawyer, and when Spencer found out I was going to him, it really pissed him off.

And I got to the point where we had the first decree, and then, God help me, I agreed to a reconciliation. Jaw said, 'You are crazy, this guy is the worst. What are you doing?' I said, 'He wants to try again, he says he has really missed me and he is sorry he has done all these things, and he is not going to see all these girls, and he definitely wants a family . . .' And so we got back together.

Well, my parents were so angry with me they could hardly speak. And as we couldn't go home for Christmas we thought we would take a cruise for a so-called second honeymoon. People that go on cruises at Christmas have really sad family lives, and, boy, we had a whole boatload of these sad types, a gay hat designer with an old lady friend of his, sweet but rather pathetic, and then us, it was like *The Love Boat** for rejects. It highlighted our isolation from the world and

* A popular US TV programme.

from any sense of community: for someone like me who is such a family orientated person, to be with all these weirdos was the opposite of what life should be, and Christmas sort of highlights these things. We pretended we had a lovely time, but it was awful really.

I took a job and the next five months I became happier as my life with him recessed, somehow, and in the spring we decided mutually it wasn't working out.

He denied the affairs right through to the bitter end, until my lawyer asked me to go through some Visa bills, and I found all the dirty weekends: two people, breakfast, lunch, dinner, Sunday newspapers, he was so cheap – he'd done all his canoodling on the company. We got the divorce on the grounds of his adultery.

I had every ground there is for marriage to be made null and void, and that was reassuring because it meant that I could go to church and receive communion; if you divorce, you can't receive sacraments, but, because it was annulled, I could walk down the aisle again – in a white dress if I chose to, in a Roman Catholic church.

People often don't learn from their mistakes. What's really frightening is that I've found myself attracted to the same kind of – shit is the word people use to describe Spencer, and those people I find interesting . . .

BARBARA

There were no problems at all. . .

We met when we were both working for the same firm; I was 34 and Billy is four years younger than I am. We had become best, best friends, more than that, soul mates, it was a very unusual, deep, successful relationship, sexually, everything – it just grew and grew, there were no problems at all. I had gone back to New York where I come from, and the person I was working for drowned suddenly, and it was a very stunning lesson, don't put off until tomorrow . . . So I immediately rang Billy and said, 'I am coming back to London,' and he picked me up at the airport, with a bottle of champagne in his hand, and he proposed.

We planned it immediately. We went to the Chelsea Registry Office, my best friend flew over from New York, and I found a fabulous wedding dress – we really looked the part.

A honeymoon didn't really seem important; we went down to Stonehenge because I had never seen it, and we drove around the countryside and stayed in country inns.

Sex tended to get in the way. Our love had been of best friends, and really Billy wanted it to remain that way, he wanted us to continue to be best friends and pals, but I was interested in a full married life.

Billy's and my relationship before we married was much more on an intellectual level, the sexual aspect had never been that important. Having lived in New York prior to moving to London I had sort of gone off sex: because I work in men's fashion a number of my close friends are gay, and I felt I was drowning in a sea of people dying of AIDS. So I had chosen to be celibate.

Well, I guess the thing to do here is to be totally honest with you, the real story, I was nervous about telling you. Billy is gay. I knew the minute I met him, I mean he is openly gay, but although I knew Billy was gay I still fell in love with him because he was the most fabulous person I'd ever met, and still is, actually. But to tell you the truth, we never had sex. We slept together and had a very supportive, emotional closeness, but never had full sex.

In the very beginning, when there was still some hope in my mind, I did gently try to initiate sex on several occasions.

Once, we were in bed together, holding each other and touching each other, and very gently I made an intimate move with my hand, and he moved my hand away, and he said, 'Look, it is just not going to work.'

I wasn't naive, thinking this was going to be a bed of roses, I knew it would be tough: but you just don't know how tough.

Because I had been celibate for four years, it was easier to bear at first. If I had come from an intensely sexual relationship to that, it might have been much more frustrating. But retrospectively I can say it is just not the natural way to be. You can choose for periods of time to be celibate, but we are all sexual beings, and when you frustrate your sexual energy you are changing something fundamental.

It slowly destroyed my confidence as a woman; when you don't feel sexually attractive to a person you love and are married to, there is this sort of dead zone where you don't really exist as a female. I came to be quite resentful at the end.

It came to an end because Billy was so miserable, and the minute he came to me and said, 'We have got to stop this charade,' I realised how miserable I was. I had been fooling myself into thinking I was happy, talking myself into the idea that things could work out.

I think it would have broken apart much sooner had he not been a very loving and caring person, I mean I never came home that there wasn't a funny card or a note, or my dinner ready if I was having a bad week at work. So there was this amazing, caring, loving, sharing relationship which up to this point in my life nobody had ever given me, but it just wasn't viable long-term.

The day I announced I was getting divorced the managing director of the company where I work invited me out to dinner. It was like being a kid, thinking it is Christmas morning and there is going to be this fabulous gift. I was nervous, but it's like riding a bicycle . . . and we have a very good sexual relationship. Initially I was much more interested in the sexual side of the relationship, and I was afraid I was overwhelming him with my sexual needs.

Now that I am no longer celibate, I realise what I was missing .

GERALD

Then we both sort of dried up, lost interest, lost desire, lost heart . . .

We met in Australia in 1963; I had just left university, I was 21, and, after three years in the rain of Cambridge, I got a job as a drama graduate teacher at Sydney University, and I was there for a year. Julia was also 21.

You know how at cocktail parties you fall in with the person you're most like – we realised that we two were from a very much paler, colder, chillier background, we were both so European in this very sun-baked setting, we were tall and ungainly and white, all the rest were in bathing suits, we were so rain-soaked and European compared to these very bronzed, fit Australians.

We both had come from families where love was not easy: my parents in many ways were wonderful parents, but not very giving in terms of affection. And we had not found very much sexual or social happiness, we hadn't had very happy love lives. I had been left by a woman I deeply loved at Cambridge, Julia had been very much in love with an Indian boy who wanted to marry her and go back to Delhi, but she decided she couldn't start a life in India. So we had both come to the end of rather tricky love affairs in which, although we had been passionately involved, we hadn't actually slept with our partners, we were both virgins.

The nature of the relationship in those early days was very polite, very formal, both of us very nervous of our bodies, but we were drawn together by a feeling of being different from the rest of them, and we began going out at night, going to restaurants, going to movies.

I can't remember many laughs, but I do remember a feeling of being very comfortable with her, I found that she was not so very different from the girls I had known at Cambridge.

And by about Christmas we realised we were very close, and that we had found, I don't know what you'd call it . . . a friendship. We were not sleeping together, but we both thought we were in love, and I think we were in love, actually. And by about June, we decided to get engaged.

I was going back to London to start a job on a newspaper, she had planned to go back to New York. We began to talk about the possibility of marriage, and how to do it geographically. Would she come to London, would I go to New York, how would we organise this? We both agreed that we weren't going to live in Australia, because that was wonderful for a year, but it really was a kind of beach, and after about a year you start saying: I have to go back to real life.

So at Christmas, she came over and stayed with my parents, and she spent a month over here and looked around, and thought yes, she could live in London, it wasn't so different from New York. And the following summer, we got married in New York, and came back to England, and that was the first time we slept together.

Sex had been quite a big issue. We weren't very agile in bed, sexually inept I think is the word for it. We talked about it all the time, it was a sort of obsession of people of my age – we all felt that we were very bad at it. Sex began in 1963: we were the transition period, we were the generation that got caught both ways, we were not quite the sixties, we were sort of late-fifties fumbling liberation. It's all in Kingsley Amis. I felt very inadequate, and I was very nervous of it, and our sex life was at first pretty bad, lack of co-ordination, lack of confidence, memories of terrible fumbling disasters as students. And then gradually we got better at it . . .

I think I underestimated how difficult it must have been for her. I mean London sort of seemed like New York, and she was indeed keen to get away from mother, and so I took it for granted that it was therefore going to be a really good life for her, but I think it wasn't. Looking back on it, I really didn't understand how traumatic the new life was for her because she covered it very well, she was very well controlled, and still is, she is a woman of extraordinary control. It has taken me twenty-five years to know how little I really know her.

I never gave her credit for coming to a new country, and marrying into a fairly difficult family. We are not difficult in that we are not alcoholic, we are not violent, but we aren't an easy family; we are noisy, we are neurotic, we are flamboyant, we are desperately ambitious, we all talk all the time, she was taking on a lot of people with me. I am one of four children, I have two parents who are very much around, I didn't have the kind of family that gracefully backed away, and the family took enormous interest in Julia, in where we were living and in our lives.

We rented a tiny flat, one room really. I began writing a book about . . . She got a job as a publisher.

And very soon we had our first child.

We bought a little house in Putney for £7,000 which I remember was the largest cheque I had ever written, and we had three or four years there, and, when our second child was born, the house got too small.

I think at that point something had already begun to go a bit wrong, but to this day I don't quite know what; quite early in the marriage we both realised that it wasn't quite right, but it wasn't bad enough to do anything about it: it wasn't disastrous, we weren't having great fights, I wasn't drinking, she wasn't unfaithful, I wasn't unfaithful – there were none of the obvious things you can pinpoint and say, This is a bad marriage.

But I am hugely unobservant, and I think I closed my eyes to certain truths. Truth number one, we were not actually very well suited back in England; we had been very well suited in Australia when we were both looking for some sort of escape, but people who marry to avoid something else don't really marry for each other. Two, we married to escape things like bachelorhood, or our own families, or being alone. Not good enough reason for two people to marry. Three, we both thought we ought to have children, Julia wanted a family, I know I did.

In the marriage there was boredom, irritability, a feeling that we neither of us really had much to say to each other unless it was about the children, a constant need to fill the house with other people, to not be alone, and gradually she became more and more introvert, more and more like the novelist she had become.

Our sex life was not good. It had been OK for a couple of years – while the children were young it was actually quite active – but then we both sort of dried up, lost interest, lost desire, lost heart, it became very mechanical, and there were actually very long gaps when we didn't go near each other at all. And therefore, when our fourth child, Jennifer, was born, we were both kind of amazed, and that seemed to sort of revive the marriage for a bit.

We moved to the country, to a big house in Haslehurst, and from then on I was always away really. I was driving to London every day, and at the weekends I began looking for reasons not to be home. What is awful is realising that you are living with somebody who you're not really with at all. We were like total strangers, we hardly communicated. I was driving back at night to sleep and getting up in the morning and going to work, and there was no reason to be there, except for the children, and they were beginning to go away to school anyway.

I didn't have an affair until quite late in the marriage; I had an affair in Washington and although the affair wasn't going to lead to anything, and I certainly didn't want it to, I suddenly realised what I was missing, which was someone to hold, someone to touch, someone to laugh with. It was a revelation. I suddenly understood about sex. I could never understand why people were so obsessed by physical love, and then I understood what it was all about, and why it mattered – it was like discovering wine, or food, or skiing, it was a whole sort of treat.

It was agony too. I didn't know what to do. I didn't know how to go home, how not to go home, how to leave.

I went home and didn't do anything, which is a typical English reaction – just abandon the whole problem. And we survived another two or three years in this increasingly awful marriage. Then I went to Boston and met Rachel who I had known for a long time because we had been together at Cambridge, and we began an affair, and this time I did tell Julia, I went back home and said to Julia, 'Look, I am having an affair, it hasn't been a good marriage for a long time, can we have a divorce?' And she more or less said no. Quite politely, but quite firmly, she said, 'I am Catholic, I don't believe in divorce, I will put up with this affair, but we are not getting divorced . . .'

I had a nasty feeling I was going to be up against the Catholic thing, that marriage is for ever. She said, 'Look, it *is* for ever, just don't have another affair and it will be all right.' And so I did what she said, not really because of that, but because of Jennifer.

I realised that I had not really been much good with the other three children, I had hardly been home when they were small, because I had been working so hard, partly to make a living and partly to avoid Julia. And I suddenly knew that, with Jennifer, this was my last chance of fatherhood, the others were suddenly teenagers, and I didn't know them, and I thought: My God, if I leave home I will never really have known my children. So quite selfishly, I gave into Julia's Catholic argument, not because I believed it, but because I didn't want to lose Jennifer.

And then, rather to my amazement, I had a complete breakdown, something which had never happened before. At 42, 43, I had a complete and utter nervous breakdown which came out of the blue – I couldn't work, I couldn't get out of bed, I mean a real, classic, old-fashioned nervous breakdown, the kind when you believe that door handles are so blazing hot you daren't touch them. Julia, being a very sensible, very practical woman, got me to a psychiatrist who immediately put me into a clinic.

Thank God for BUPA, because I could never have otherwise afforded it.

Anyway, I then got better, and went back to work, still living with Julia. About another two years went by, and I realised I couldn't do it, I couldn't stay at home. And, if you can believe it, I then had another nervous breakdown. Having had one trying to stay, I then had my second one trying to leave. And I went through exactly the same thing: couldn't work, couldn't function, back into the clinic. But this time, when I came out I didn't go back home at all, I rented a flat in London, and began the whole manoeuvre of divorce.

I went to Julia, and said, 'I can't go on with this marriage, we have got to get divorced. I know it's against your Catholic religion, but if we don't get divorced I'm going to finish up in a mental home for the rest of my life, and we can't afford it.' And she saw that I was right, and she realised something had to be done.

So we agreed to separate.

Once divorce proceedings started I felt relieved and guilty in about equal measure really.

I blame myself a lot. I think if you do a guilt quotient, I was a far worse husband, and she was in many ways a very good wife. She was loyal, she was absolutely faithful until the very end, and then she had her first affair when I was already half-way out of the door. I think she is still rather more traumatised than I am, but that's to do with her

Catholic childhood. It's been very tough on her.

I've paid a price for it, and the price I've paid is not seeing my youngest as often as I would have liked, she still lives with her mother. And my parents and I are now more distant because they are close to Julia, and they feel that I should have stuck at the marriage. Even though they knew it was not good, they feel I kind of chickened out. And in a funny way, men aren't supposed to go, I felt it was ungallant to leave, it was kind of rude to leave, and on the other hand I kind of had to . . .

Then of course there is all the sorting out of what to do about the house and how to organise the money.

I still pay a £1,000 a month alimony, which I've always agreed to do, and we occasionally have one or two arguments, we're bickering at the moment about pension rights: the issue is, do you cash in the pension funds before they fall due, or do you keep them in the bank until they make more money. It's a fairly minor quibble.

But now it all seems very dead really. I see Julia about once a month.

She's found a man, near where she lives, which is lovely if it works, he is an executive in IBM, or ICI, IBM, I think. She said to me the other day, 'For the first time, I think I've found somebody I really love.' You always assume that people find in their second marriages what they haven't found in the first, so I asked her to go on, and she said, 'Well, he's very quiet and he thinks a lot and he's very undemanding.' And I thought: I suppose I was rather demanding in a way, I am quite hard to live with.

I hope it works out, because she's 50, and it is quite tough for a woman on her own, I think men have a much easier time.

I actually like being alone; when Rachel's not here I lead a very happy bachelor life, I go to dinner parties, I go to the theatre, and I am actually very content. I am rather worried by how happy I am on my own, which is now a problem because Rachel wants to marry again, and I really don't, and that's going to be quite a trauma this summer. She is now 47 or 48, and she really wants a second marriage. Rachel spends half the year in England, and half in Italy, so I have a deep and loving and quite good sexual life with her for about half the year, but for half the year I can write my books and travel, and there is something to be said for having the bachelor life back, especially if you haven't had it, because I got married very young, I was a father by the time I was 24.

I very much want not to lose her, but I also want very much not to marry her, and she is at that point where I think she feels if she's going to make the second half of her life work she'd better find a marriage. She is very open about it, she makes it very clear she wants to get married.

And I think I am not a very marriageable kind of man, I'm now beginning to think that I was never a very good prospect as a husband, that I am somehow too selfish, my attention span is not very long, I like change. Rachel always says that one of the things about me she finds most irritating is that I am at my best in crowded rooms, at cocktail parties, talking to strangers, and it's true, in a funny way, I like performing for strangers, I don't like people getting too close. I have a lot of friends who I literally see about twice a year, and Rachel says, 'How can you regard them as friends when you only see them for two days a year?' And I say, 'Yes, but that is what I call friendship.' I like distant relationships, and that is probably not a very good basis for a marriage . . .

RACHEL

The point at which I discovered that other men were interested in me was very exciting, I think in some ways it was as sexually exciting as the sex. It did an enormous amount for my self-confidence . . .

I never believed it would be so painful.

We were young together, and I think that makes a huge difference; whatever relationships or marriages one forms in maturity, they're never quite like being young together, discovering the world, becoming successful together. The pain comes from a severing of ties which go back a long way, to a time when we really didn't have any other ties, we just had each other.

My husband and I had a long, twenty-year marriage, which was more a friendship, I suppose, than a great passion. We became friends and then we married. It wasn't ever a passionate affair, there wasn't a sexual spark – for either of us, actually – but we were very compatible.

At some point Rupert decided he wanted me, and he laid siege to me, he was absolutely determined I would marry him. My husband was a man who didn't make many decisions, he left most decisions over twenty years to me. But he was a man who, when he decided he wanted something, wanted it to the exclusion of everything else. I wasn't very interested in being married, I didn't have any romantic notions of being married. Until I got into my present relationship, I had no idea of what romantic love was like.

I think Rupert wanted me as a complement to his personality. He is the kind of person who can make himself absolutely invisible, as I can't. When he enters a room, the dynamic of the room doesn't change. When I enter a room it does. And that's what he wanted. In exchange, he was willing to put up with the very unconventional woman he found, and to be more of a wife than a husband.

For example, he would arrange the dinner parties, keep in touch with family and friends. I was broadstrokes, he was details. I'm very good with machines and money, he is good at things like laundry and cooking. And although I think in some ways he would have liked a more traditional wife, he was certainly more than willing to put up with a nontraditional wife in order to have me.

'If you don't marry me, I'll take this job in Paris,' he would say. It was quite direct. And I said, 'Don't be silly. We're fine the way we are, let's just leave it.' And he'd say, 'If you don't marry me, I'll take this job in Paris . . .' And my sister said, 'He'll do it.' I said, 'No, he won't. He loves me, he's not going anywhere.' And he took the job in Paris, at which point I thought we really had too much together for me to give this up. And I said, 'All right, all right, all right, I'll marry you.' It wasn't on my part an enthusiastic choice for marriage, it was: I love this man, and I would like to live with him, and if that's the price, that's the price.

Anybody who thinks honeymoons are a good idea is nuts. We went to the South of France, we took a villa above Menton. It was perfectly beautiful. And it was a sexual nightmare, and in some ways it was one of the most destructive two weeks of my life.

We were suddenly, after having been very comfortable together, very uncomfortable together, and I felt very trapped, and he felt terribly frightened.

My husband, it turned out, had had an appalling sexual history before me, which was a mainly impotent life. He had tried very hard to fix it, and indeed we tried very hard to fix it at various points during our marriage, and it was not the key, I believe, to the break-up of our marriage at all. We had lived together for several months before he went to Paris, and had assembled something of a sex life; then he went to Paris and didn't come back until we actually got married, so the honeymoon was really the first time we were together for more than six months. And it had somehow gone, it was like a trick that he had remembered briefly that went away again. And it never really came back, I mean my husband was impotent for most of our marriage, virtually all of it. We certainly did try, we had two fairly long bouts of sex therapy, at the end of which I said this is too cruel, this is too painful, let's not do this any more.

Virtually every sexual relationship I have ever had has been with a man who has first been my friend, so I kind of assumed that that was the way it was going to be with us, and it would grow, but it didn't. What happened was the friendship grew, the trust grew, the dependency grew, my husband was very dependent on me for our whole marriage, but the intimacy didn't grow, and the sexual compatibility didn't grow.

We learned to talk a bit about it, but there isn't very much point in talking about it if you can't actually fix it, and at a certain point we simply stopped trying to fix it, and we stopped trying to do it, and that solved a lot of problems.

Things didn't get better until we had a place to live, until some of the uncertainties about our life had gone away; he was working, I was working, money was coming in, we had a place to live, we had friends, and there were some very good years.

He was always enormously supportive to me, and I gave him a stability he had never had – we were a great team: we may not have been a marriage, but we were a hell of a team.

I think I was always aware that we lacked an emotional intimacy. We were too polite to each other. I would try and provoke rows all the time in the early days, but it's very hard to argue with somebody who won't argue with you. And it became clear that the ease of living together didn't alleviate the sexual tension at all.

A woman who is married to a man who doesn't want her physically feels unlovely. I wasn't a beautiful girl, I was the kind of girl about whom people say she's got a lovely personality. I was never anybody's first choice until I was Rupert's first choice, and I was absolutely without question his first choice. But the point at which I discovered that other men were interested in me was very exciting, I think in some ways it was as sexually exciting as the sex. It did an enormous amount for my self-confidence.

There is a way that a sexually active man looks at a woman, shakes hands with a woman, I am not sure I can define it to a man, but every woman knows. It's how you tell the difference between men who are straight and men who are gay, they simply look at you differently, it's to do with the tail feathers ruffling, it's to do with peeing in each corner of the garden, it's that kind of territorial showing off that men and women do for each other.

I met a great many men in the course of my work. Those in whom I was interested tended to be people who were fairly powerful individuals, I don't mean in financial terms, but strong men. My husband is mentally very fragile, he is damaged desperately by an appalling childhood, and I always had to be very careful about what I said and how I said it; therefore powerful men who actually couldn't be hurt like that were very attractive to me.

I think, had I found the right lover, I would have been willing to stay married, and been enthusiastic about staying married to Rupert for ever. I have no particular moral aversion or objection to having affairs.

Until Gerald: if Gerald hadn't been so absolutely adamant that he wanted a life with me, and if I hadn't loved him so much.

We had known each other at Cambridge, and always remained friends, there was never a point in thirty years that we were not in touch.

About six years ago, Gerald said, 'I have decided that I am not going to die without telling you this: which is that I love you, I have always loved you, and I am not going to finish my life without you.' To which I said, predictably, 'Don't be silly, you are married, you have three children, this is a crazy idea, do you want to have an affair?' thinking: That will fix him, no trouble. And he said, 'No, I don't want to have an affair with you, I want to marry you.' And I said, 'This is a daft idea, you will get over it.' Well, he wouldn't go away, and he started writing to me, and he wrote to me every day for months and months and months, and what he was trying to convince me of he finally did convince me of, and I thought it was a really lousy idea.

So finally that Christmas I said, 'If you think I am giving up the best friend I have got in favour of another lover, you are very much mistaken, this is not what I want, we will have an affair.' So we did, and of course it was wonderful. At which point it then became an obsession with Gerald, I couldn't shift him. I told him, I have a very comfortable life, I like my husband – I love you – but I like my husband, and I really don't want to destroy the whole structure that we have built together.

But Gerald was very persuasive, and eventually we bought a flat together and moved in. Rupert and I were living in separate cities by now because of our work. And Rupert would come and stay with us.

I tried to talk to Rupert. I said, 'Gerald and I live together, we are more married than you and I have ever been, you do understand this, don't you?' I tried to get him to focus on it, but he wouldn't deal with it at all. There was never a point when I could get him to acknowledge the fact that I, his wife, was living with another man.

Until a year ago. My husband came over to spend Christmas with us. And on Boxing Day, I heard the telephone go, and I went downstairs, it was four o'clock in the morning, and I said, 'What on earth are you doing?' And it was Rupert, and he said, 'I am trying to make a reservation, I want to go home, I don't feel comfortable here, this place is full of you and Gerald, every invitation, every Christmas card, is you as a couple, and I want to leave.' And I said, 'Darling, you have known for years that we were together.' 'I didn't realise it . . .' So we talked for a very long time, and from that moment to this he has never wavered in his determination to get as far away from me as possible.

I had always said to him if either of us ever wanted a divorce there would be no discussion. I had hoped that maybe he would find somebody with whom he could function sexually – unlike me, he was not a man who could have an affair. And so if he did find someone, I wanted him to know he was free to go to them. And we did re-examine our marriage very often.

But I think part of the pain I feel with this divorce has to do with the shock, just as I didn't believe he was going to Paris at the beginning, I didn't ever think it would be Rupert who would want a divorce. But when he said he wanted it there was no choice but to say of course.

Rupert's anger with me took the form of claiming everything we owned belonged to him: I want everything. He behaved like an aggrieved wife, he behaved exactly the way Gerald's wife Julia behaved. I wouldn't allow my lawyer to take Rupert to court for my share of the property. If I am going to be divorced, which I obviously am, I am going to do it without a cat fight, and Rupert knows me well enough that I would do exactly that, and he has taken appalling advantage of it.

I have suggested on a number of occasions we should get together and talk, but Rupert doesn't want to see me. It's clear that, once we are divorced, we will have no more relationship. My pain has to do with the loss of one of the best friends I ever had, we shared so much that the loss of this marriage is like somebody dying.

To put it crudely, I don't think Rupert will marry again unless he finds somebody he can get it up for. I don't think he will put himself through that again, and nor should he. I have always believed that, if

Rupert lives with someone again, it will be with a man and not a woman. I think he is gay, but I don't think he has ever slept with a man, I think he would be as worried about his impotence in one direction as in another.

But I think he is far too conventional to come out. I once said to him, 'It doesn't matter if it is a man or a woman; love is very precious and rare – take it where you find it.'

As for me, I think Gerald will bully me until I marry him.

RICHARD

Being a doctor with hundreds of patients going through marital stress, one realises very well that communication is nearly always the fundamental problem . . .

We went out for three years, and the first time we argued was over the arrangements for getting married. I wanted a small, quiet event, in many ways like my character, I guess. She wanted the big London scene.

I thought I'd be listened to. I thought my views would be of interest, bearing in mind I was vaguely involved. Wedding lists, for example, I have always had a pathological loathing for, thinking of them as horrendously materialistic; I understand the value of them in a post-war England when people hadn't got much, but in this day and age I just don't like them, but again I was overridden.

She was tough and hard, she had a very determined streak which I hadn't seen before.

I was working pretty long hours as a junior hospital doctor, doing the standard 120 hours a week, being paid a charitable salary plus luncheon vouchers, and you tended to be on the tired side when you got home, so I didn't talk things out. Things went into a blur, I mean if you are working a one-in-two rota at a hospital, and you are only home two or three nights a week, time goes by very fast, and things happen almost before you've had a chance to blink.

I was either at work, or else we were out with friends, or seeing her parents; there was very little time alone, there was very little communication going on. Looking back ten years later, and being a doctor with hundreds of patients going through marital stress, one realises very well that communication is nearly always the fundamental problem – communication or sex.

One weekend I went back to Charlotte and said, 'We have different perceptions on what the whole thing is about, I want to delay it, for a year or two years or whatever, but I just don't want to go through with it at the moment.' And I was persuaded by her that it would be OK on the night-type thing, and that *she* was under pressure, and was just trying to keep everybody happy.

Well, I suppose everybody would say it went beautifully, personally I never felt part of it, I felt, to use a word that one learns in psychiatry, depersonalised, as if I was looking down a long tunnel at two strangers getting married.

I felt very daunted by the whole thing, it was very big and very social, and I had to make some stupid bloody speech: it wasn't the sort of wedding I would have wanted.

When we came back from our honeymoon her parents were insistent that she live in a smart part of London, and, as I was not financially able to buy a flat in Chelsea, they bought us one and did it up, which was very nice, but one naturally felt a bit emasculated by that.

I felt if she wanted to get married to me she could bloody well live where we could afford to live, not some smarty-pants place that wasn't mine or anything to do with me.

And then one night I came home, and she suddenly announced, 'I want you to leave.' I wasn't sure whether she meant leave the room or what, and I said, 'Leave where, do you want me to go upstairs?' She said, 'No, no, I want you to leave the flat.' She'd had enough, she said, she wasn't happy, this wasn't the sort of life she wanted, and she didn't like being married to someone who was never there. And that was it, she refused to discuss it any further, just repeated she wanted me to leave the next day.

Anyway, I went to work the next morning – maybe I shouldn't have done, but you can't not turn up, and when I came back two nights later, because I was on duty the following night, I found all my stuff packed up in boxes by the front door, and a note saying 'Please leave the keys when you leave'. We'd been married five months.

She went to stay with her parents, and they wouldn't let me see her, and I lived in the hospital – I don't think anybody at work ever knew what was going on; they didn't know whether I was on call or not on call, and I suppose I withdrew into a very serious shell and made no attempt to see other people, because that's the way I am.

I was never able to get near her, and she wouldn't discuss it – she's never to this day discussed it, which is unbelievable.

It is very difficult to describe ten years later the injustice of never having an explanation, not being able to talk about it, I have found it incredibly hard to take.

It doesn't make you very confident. Lack of trust, hurt, loss of confidence, loss of direction at work, loss of direction in life, obviously I still suffer from those, maybe I had them before, I don't know.

I did speak to her once on the telephone, which was the only way I could get hold of her, and she would never offer anything, she just said, 'I made a mistake, I'm very sorry, but you've got to face it.' Her tone of voice implied it was my fault, I had failed her.

She was engaged before we were divorced, she remarried as soon as she could.

I have written to her on two or three occasions when I've been deeply involved with somebody else, 'Look, I'd just like to meet and have dinner and have a talk, just to clear an unresolved conflict, it would be very helpful . . .' I've never had a reply to any of those letters.

I nearly got married again a couple of years ago, in fact that didn't happen, but I wanted to talk to Charlotte before I got engaged again, to clear the air and let her know what I was doing, out of courtesy, and also to answer a few questions.

I don't think I've ever demanded very much, considering the shock of the whole thing really, all I've ever wanted was one quiet dinner. There's no way I'd ever do anything to her other than talk. I just want to try and sort it out. It would be nice to have a resolution to things prior to making the same move again.

Ten years later, every day of the week I go on questioning why it happened: there's no doubt it still casts a shadow, I imagine it will always cast a shadow, it will probably be unresolved always, because there isn't a way of resolving it unless you discuss it, and you can't discuss it with a person who refuses to talk to you; it may seem ridiculous to her ten years later, but if she can't see that it still hurts that is a bit of a pity.

I don't like talking about it, I almost didn't come tonight, because it doesn't help me to think about it, frankly. I will probably have quite a sleepless night tonight, I should imagine it will stir up quite a lot of thoughts.

NICHOLAS

She denied everything the whole time; she played it as if I had gone mad. This I found very disturbing because I was slightly mad . . . it wasn't a rational period at all . . .

She was introduced to me by somebody who said, 'I think you will like this lady . . .'

It was a supper party, which didn't go all that well because I was exhausted, it happened to have been a very busy day at the hospital. The people who were giving her a lift after the supper were driving the wrong way, and I blew my horn to put them on the right road, and, as I looked up to wave goodbye, there was a look out of the window, and it was the eyes that did it: from the flash of those eyes I was a goner, overwhelmingly in love. I rang my friend the next day and said, 'What's the telephone number of that girl?' I then had one of the most embarrassing telephone calls of my life. I remember having to steal away from the clinic into a little room where there was a phone, and being terrified that someone would come in and listen to me: I was so keyed up that I was incredibly gauche, and everything I said came out wrong.

Because she was a beautiful actress I thought she must be very sophisticated and would have visited every swank restaurant in London, and I decided to take her home and cook her an omelette; she meanwhile was busy thinking: Great, I haven't been taken out to a decent meal for ages, but anyway, she got the omelette.

The evening went very well, a lot of talk.

I took her home and we had a kiss at the gate; I was deliberately not rushing it, because it was so precious I didn't want to sully it with a quick whatsit.

I hadn't ever met anybody quite so positively revelling in life. The fantastic thing about Cordelia was that here was somebody who physically turned me on enormously, and was a good, deep thinker, she was very well read and had a very interesting view on life that was totally novel to me. I had always been interested in the arts and theatre, but this was somebody who was really involved in it.

I then went away to Africa for three weeks on some scholarship and I missed her greatly and spent my whole time rushing up and down to post offices and poste restantes. I was pretty sure that this was it.

I came back and she had done lots of sweet things; she had fixed a sunroof on my crappy old car to turn it into something that wasn't quite so crappy, which was a very sweet thing to think of, a very ungirly thing, and it was expensive and she hadn't got any money: we were both pretty in love, I think.

Cordelia had a very busy career so we rarely took holidays. She was always working and I was always working and we never coincided. We went on one pretty dreadful holiday, and the house we were staying in was so awful that this inhibited us and we didn't make love; we were both pleased to get home and made love, I remember, pretty spectacularly, and that was almost certainly the conceptual love-making, because I then had to go away on a conference, so that pretty spectacular love-making resulted in this delicious child. It is quite nice to think back on, there must be lots of people who conceive a child and have no memory of that, 'got 'twixt wake and sleep', but this child: there was 'sport at his making'.

She was terribly brave and good about the pregnancy, very happy and very health-conscious, and I am sure that made the little lad as happy and healthy as he is – and he is pretty smashing.

Cordelia landed two wonderful parts at the National and then the theatre closed. And that was a blow for her, and she started taking anything, and I remember telling her I didn't think some of the parts were worth doing and she should wait for something really good. And I turned out to be right, good things were offered, but she was already doing things, and the worst thing you can ever be is an advising husband who is right, and I think that put a bit of tension in the air.

And then she did a fringe revue, and there was a fella in it – and I knew immediately something was happening, I suppose because I am a doctor my job is to suss things out very quickly. But I think by my diagnosing it, possibly before it had been a physical relationship, I perhaps pushed it into becoming one. And I rather overdid my jealousy too, I said some pretty nasty things, and I probably killed her love for me.

I then started wondering about everything she did. Once she came back at 4 a.m., and I pretended to be asleep. When she got into bed she said, 'Go to sleep, love, it's only twelve-thirty,' so I knew that was a lie.

She denied everything the whole time; she played it as if I had gone mad. This I found very disturbing because I was slightly mad . . . it wasn't a rational period at all.

My jealousy got pretty destructive and I moved out for a couple of weeks to try to cool down, leaving her with the child – and still going with this chap.

I felt very emotional about it, I felt she had been contaminated: I think a lot of chaps do get upset if somebody else has been near their property, which is ridiculous really, but there you are. I thought a lot about sex and I thought an awful lot about him, he was black which is always a bit of a threat to a white man, and I was sexually very jealous.

I had to go away to give a lecture, and I rang from my hotel room and said, 'You are not going to have an affair with him, are you?' And she said, 'You can't stop me.' I didn't sleep that night, I remember walking around Stratford-upon-Avon all night, and watching the swans wake up in the morning.

I think if I had been cool for about three weeks it would have all blown over because the fella she was keen on was obviously a fairly uninteresting chap in lots of ways – no disrespect to him. And if I hadn't overreacted I would still be living with my son: you see, at the end of the day I no longer live with my son, and I regret that very deeply.

I wasn't sleeping. I told the GP, 'I think Cordelia is having an affair, and I haven't slept for forty-eight hours.' 'Oh dear,' she said, 'how terrible.'

I didn't eat and lost weight, and a lot of hair fell out, it was telium effluvium, I mean I knew what it was, I could diagnose myself, but it didn't stop it being frightening; at least I knew I wasn't going to go bald.

I didn't miss a single clinic but I was close to it, and on top of that I was giving these wretched lectures; funnily enough I'd given a lecture when I literally hadn't slept for two nights and I was virtually unconscious, and I sat down at the end of it, and one of my co-consultants said, 'God, I have never heard you lecture so well, that was really good.'

The play ended and he moved to another theatre. I had to go away for a couple of days to give a lecture somewhere and when I came back I realised she'd been to see him, and that distressed me very very considerably.

She never apologised and that really was a big problem for me. If only she had said, 'I am sorry, love, let's have another go,' I was still in love, but she never ever did.

We started to take a few delicate steps towards going right, and we were getting closer together, we started making love again – all those things which had been pretty difficult for a while, and then she was offered a part touring, and it was eighteen months away. I said, 'If you do that, there is no way we will get better.' She said, 'I'll come home every weekend . . .' but every weekend was spent moving from Hull to Nottingham, Nottingham to Lincoln. I suppose she was miserable, and she then fell for another chap in this new company.

It was the tone of her voice on the phone, I said, 'Good God, there is somebody else, isn't there?' and she said, 'Yes . . .'

ELIZABETH

We had just built a conservatory. I think a conservatory is always a very bad sign in a marriage; the minute one says we must have a conservatory, something is wrong, because nobody needs a conservatory, and people build them because they feel they need some sort of displacement activity, like having another baby . . .

I think that when you are ready to get married you are like a plum on a tree, and the first person who comes along and shakes it, you drop off: it's to do with the timing as much as the person.

In a marriage you have troughs and heights and the relationship changes all the time – it simply goes on too long. My theory is that however good a relationship is there is nobody in the whole world one can live with for longer than about twelve years; in the end twelve years is as much as one really wants of one person in your life.

And after about twelve or thirteen years it was sort of petering out, all sorts of small things, like wearing a bath hat instead of putting your hair up, or, if you are both at a party and they're talking to somebody, you no longer listen to what they are saying.

We were living in a great big posh house and we had just built a conservatory. I think a conservatory is always a very bad sign in a marriage; the minute one says we must have a conservatory, something is wrong, because nobody needs a conservatory, and people build them because they feel they need some sort of displacement activity, like having another baby. A conservatory suggests this wonderful idealised life where you are going to sit on a rattan seat surrounded by nodding palms, but actually nobody sits around in conservatories, you sit in kitchens and leaning on the edges of things.

I met Leo at a party one evening; and a very strange thing happened, it was as if my soul had left me and gone into this other person. He was like a soul mate, he was my thoughts, he was my feelings, it was like finding me, and if that happens it is very difficult to resist – I didn't anyway; of course I should have because it is a dreadful thing to do and I shall feel ghastly and guilty about it until I die, but I was then just an empty person in my marriage, I was a husk.

I was a hopeless adulteress because I am terribly transparent, and I can't keep secrets, and I was discovered very quickly, and the whole marriage crumbled very fast; it is very much like a building collapsing, you can't stop it, it has a remorseless course, and it literally falls around you, you can't even sit up because you are covered in the rubble. And of course it's appallingly traumatic because it's not just your husband, it's two children, a large house and everything – a whole life. And the process of dismantling a whole life together and causing pain and distress to children is just as bad for both of you, even if you are the one who's initiated it and fallen in love with somebody else.

It is a period of total madness, you go sort of insane, and you drink, and you stay up until four in the morning, and you have periods where you come back together again. You cling to friends who have gone through the same things themselves, and they are the only ones who can help you, because people who are happily married aren't any use at all. It is all very intense, and you are always crying and you both get terribly thin, and it is very hard just to concentrate on the normal things like getting the children from school or whatever.

It was so terribly emotional – and passionate – it was wonderful in a way, I remember we went to Paris when I knew I was leaving, but he didn't really know, and we made love all night, I mean literally until dawn, which we hadn't done for years. I could still see what I had seen in my husband, and that, if it was the other way around, and I had been married for twelve years to Leo, I would have fallen passionately in love with Gordon.

But I can't be with two people at the same time, I am totally monogamous.

The suffering of your husband is as nothing to the guilt you feel about children. Actually they are more resilient than one thinks; I remember I was driving from somewhere in the country back to London with them and I knew at some point on this journey I had got to tell them we were going to split up. And I saw this layby with a transport café, and I pulled into it, and I said, 'I have to tell you: Daddy and I are going to split up' – and they both burst into tears, and I remember sitting on this windswept dual carriageway, all of us crying and crying, it was just too awful, I can hardly bear to think about it. But then a mile or so later they were badgering me to get some crisps, and they were talking about themselves, children are totally egocentric; of course they are not interested in how we are feeling or what is happening in our lives, they are only thinking about their own concerns, which is as it should be.

So after I had done this one ghastly, selfish act of my whole life, we both said from now on we must only think about what to do to make it all right for the children, to be totally unselfish from then onwards. We agreed we would never say anything about each other in front of the children, so all our ghastly things were said behind closed doors when the children weren't there.

I never asked Gordon for any money – we just sold the house and split it in half. We divided things up, doing this terrible thing of going round the house with little stickers, blue stickers for him and red for me. We did it in a spirit of terrible sadness, but working at it together. It was rather touching really because we were actually being very nice to each other, saying, 'Look, why don't *you* have this because you have always liked it.' And we got together packages for our next life, like when you go to a holiday place and they give you a little starter pack of two hard boiled eggs and a Nescafé; I gave him a starter pack of cookery books because he can't cook, and he gave me one of household tools because I am hopeless around the house.

There were various preparations, like for a death in a way, I got things in order, and I timed it so that I moved out when the children were away for a week's holiday at camp.

We decided to move near to each other so the children could move from one house to the other without having to take buses or be driven, otherwise they would be children with carrier bags.

Gordon thought he might as well get somebody gorgeous to keep up his morale, so he got a very beautiful Icelandic girl to come and be our au pair, which was a farce because she was so beautiful she spent the whole time with hoards and hoards of men having this wonderful time and totally neglecting the children, and she would braid her thick blonde hair all day in tiny little plaits while my daughter would go about with her hair sticky and unbrushed.

The awful thing is I now can't see what the marriage was all about.

It's partly because one changes so much. When you are married you are constantly compromising to suit each other, for instance, the way we did up our houses: I'd go to his house and it wouldn't be at all like I would do it, and I'm sure he feels the same about mine. Before, if he liked a picture of this or that, I'd put it up, but the minute you're on your own, you realise that you have been trying to suit each other, and when you spring apart it is as if you've been tied together by rubber bands, you spring much further apart than you realise. Even figures of speech that the other person uses they wouldn't have used when they were with you, and they start going to films that you wouldn't want to see, and that intensifies a feeling that you didn't have nearly as much in common as you thought.

I am very different with Leo. I am not a wife, and you are a very different person if you are not a wife, because you are not talking about anything to do with domesticity or children or arrangements. I am not very good at being domestic, it is so boring. If I have to talk to somebody about what I'm going to buy at Sainsbury's I start resenting them. So it's not like a marriage at all, I would never marry him, he's something that isn't to do with marriage, domesticity would destroy the relationship.

I have a very separate life with the children and I don't want somebody else coming in because it muddies the equation. He may come for supper and stay the night, but it's not his place, he has a toothbrush, but that's about it.

ARTHUR

She smashed my glasses at one point, and she slammed a door so it cut me heavily on the face, and I was pouring blood. And I went into the bathroom and locked the door, and she stood outside, violently kicking the door, on and on and on and on, but without saying anything . . .

In 1960 I was director of the Nottingham Theatre Festival, which was then quite a lively sort of miniature Chichester. I needed a leading lady, and several names were put forward to me, including an American who I hadn't heard of before, and her name was Gail Buchanan. I remember the audition now; she wasn't a frightfully good actress but she had enormous personality, enormous character. There was a shortlist of about three and I finally decided to offer her the job. She wasn't at all liked by the other women in the company, but I thought she had a marvellous brash vigour, which was so different from the English bourgeois middle-class gentility I was brought up in, and this was very attractive indeed.

I was attracted to her right away, and an affair started during the season. She had left her husband and her daughter in America in order to come to England and further her career, and she had come with a lover too, who was pursuing her, and would come up to Nottingham every now and again. One night I was with Gail, and I woke up to hear him knocking on the door. The only way out was through the bathroom window, which was about nine inches by eighteen inches, so while Gail was pretending to have difficulty opening the front door, as in a good Feydeau, I was literally struggling out of this tiny hole – all of which we regarded as immense fun. At the end of the season we started to share a flat, and he still didn't know we were living together, and he rang me one day and said, 'Can you cast any light on this . . . ?' and to my shame I evaded telling him, but I did a bit later.

She wasn't really a very good actress. She more or less demanded parts from me as a right, she would get my scripts and read them and say, 'That is what I want to play . . .' She felt she deserved it, somehow, it was her due. Once or twice I cast her for things in my own productions for which she was not really suitable at all; it did mean that one cut some fairly sharp corners in casting to keep her in work. She was a gut actress, it all came from instinct, and so parts like Pegeen Mike (in *Playboy of the Western World*) who is a wild Irish girl she was fine for, but she couldn't act comedy. Parts such as Bernard Shaw's *Candida*, which calls for comic instinct as well as comic craft, she couldn't get the hang of at all. She seemed to be unable to get work outside what I could give her, or very little – when it came to the divorce I actually had to add up for my solicitor how many parts she had played, and how many of those I had been responsible for, because she was claiming I had given her no help in her career, and I had to prove in the nasty way one has to in a divorce that that wasn't true, and it turned out to be thirty-four parts in total, of which I cast her for twenty-nine.

So I cast her when I could and there would sometimes be terrible, terrible rows when I knew she was really totally unsuitable for something, and I would be hauled over the coals for casting someone who would be so totally wrong. She accepted that then, but by God it was a tough fight.

She would dramatise everything. It was a regular thing to turn every departure into a drama: if she was going somewhere she would leave it until the last possible moment before getting ready, and then go at it as if it was a great crisis, absolutely tear around the house, and drive the car away at enormous speed and squeal of brakes, none of which was necessary if she had started quarter of an hour earlier.

On the evening of our wedding day, Gail and I went to the open air theatre in Regent's Park. It began to rain half-way through and so the show was abandoned. Now, I do not know to this day whether the following was manufactured by her or not, but when we got home she noticed she had lost her wedding ring. There were horrors and shocks, and we went back the following morning, and, lo and behold, she found it, *there* it was – and this was a tremendously good omen for our marriage. Now, she was made in such a way that she could well have done that as a little act, because she was full of putting melodrama into everything, and I still don't know whether it was real or not.

I went to do a season at Plymouth, and she was determined to play Ibsen's *The Doll's House.* She was very pregnant, and our son Jamie was born during the rehearsals. Jamie is the great bond in our life still, he was always the great strength, and we both love him, and he was used very deliberately by her as an emotional pawn during the divorce, which was three and a half years of great savagery when it happened, but he has always been the best possible thing that emerged from those years.

We tried to have another child, but she couldn't get a second pregnancy, and we then decided to adopt. Gail was taken by the idea of adopting a coloured child. She was very clear as to what she wanted, she wanted a round child, a round, dark or brown child, not a pointy child like an Arab or an Indian. So we found an organisation which dealt with cross-race adoption, and started the process of looking into adopting another child. A Miss Doherty rang us up one day and said, 'There is a boy called Edward, Edward Tomlin, who I think you will like, and he is just over a year old, will you come and see him?' To this day I swear she then gave me a description of our own child Jamie: she said, 'He is very forthright, a leader, and always up to larks and climbing trees . . .' which in fact was all the things that Edward wasn't.

We went to see Eddie, and there was this small, round boy with a runny nose, who didn't actually speak, and wasn't out of nappies, but he seemed decent enough. And we went over on weekends for many weeks to see him and have long walks with him, and he never uttered a single word throughout all the time. On one occasion, Miss Doherty was driving us back to the station, and she said, 'What does he call you?' I said, 'He hasn't actually uttered yet,' and she said, 'Well, is it all right if he calls you Daddy?' I should have been on my guard, but there wasn't any reason to be, because the bond was growing, and we wanted a child.

And so we slid into an adoption. Perhaps we should have taken more time, perhaps we should have looked elsewhere, but there he was, fate had thrown us together. And that was it, we fostered him for six months, and then legally adopted him, which was quite a short procedure, in chambers with a magistrate.

Gail then had a lovely fashion accessory, a black and a white child, and she absolutely loved the drama of this.

But when she had to deal with the problems of being tied with two children, it was all the things she didn't want. And then all the problems started with Eddie, because Eddie turned out to be absolutely without any initiative at all, really thick – although very dear, and with great affection. It was his character. He was so unrewarding and so unlike us; we were a fairly quick lot, nerve-edge stuff, and he was the very opposite. A typical situation would be where we'd go to the beach, and Jamie would rush off and build sandcastles and get shells, and Edward would just sit with his mouth literally hanging open, and his nose running, staring into the middle distance. Gail would get very angry and say, 'It's him or me' – she said that several times. She suddenly felt she had given up what she regarded as a very promising career to look after a child who wasn't rewarding. Edward, I am afraid, was a big factor in the break-up, because she felt that her life had been much diminished by him.

Then there was the business of special schools, and as a result we were always strapped for cash, we were always dangling on the edge of a major overdraft, and it was 'his fault', because, if we hadn't adopted him, there would have been enough to go around.

Gail was always very jealous of my career, which was going well, and tried to claim credit for it. She was always telling people she'd thought up the plots for my plays, and gave me the best ideas on how to write scenes and so on, which was a bit sad and desperate, because often her ideas were good, but she wanted to claim the credit for it all, as if I was her creation in some curious way.

She would never let me go to a lunch or dinner party by myself: if I was seeing somebody interesting in connection with work, she had to be there. In many ways I was glad to have her there, but she had to come and perform. She used to take over, it was intolerable; she would assume that she was the centre of the evening, as if she were Joan Collins or Elizabeth Taylor, and would tell naughty stories, and be very dominant and noisy. I didn't realise just how polite the English are, because I thought they all loved it, and in fact they all hated it, and they told me after the marriage was over: 'We couldn't have stood another night with your wife at our dinner table.'

One thing I felt resentful about: there was a small group of directors who were invited to meet Marlon Brando, who was my great hero, we were going to have lunch with him – wives weren't invited. And Gail absolutely insisted that she should come, and she proceeded to make my life an absolute misery because I hadn't said to the host that I must bring my wife. And eventually, in order to make life bearable, I had to cancel my going, so I never did meet him.

Things got worse and worse, and more and more violent: slamming doors, throwing things, screaming, having hysterics, jumping about the place. Towards the end, some struggling, which she initiated. I would want to get out of the room, and she would stand in the doorway and say, 'No, you're not going . . .' but not really having anything to say. And then I'd try and get out, and she'd grab hold of me, and I'd grab hold of her, it was all frightfully undignified and stupid.

She used to throw things in fights. She took a delight in throwing crockery, and if I got angry she would pick up a kitchen knife – pretend to be defending herself. I hadn't a thought of charging at her, but she liked to hype up the vibes like that.

Yes, we still had good things, but the number of bad things was starting to exceed them by far, and my blood pressure had really started to become a problem.

She was getting very strange, she would start weeping, shaking, going white, and clutching the furniture: but I never knew whether it was a drama like all the other dramas – it always happened in front of other people. It was all so overdone: could it have been calculated?

She was always tremendously confident that her power over me was so strong that I would never leave her. But I knew this was the beginning of the end: although it may take years, I knew we were on the way out.

There was one last terrible, terrible scene. We had booked sometime before to go to Madrid, and I knew that I had to tell her then that there was going to be no more.

We went to Madrid and saw the sights, and went a lot to the Prado. And that is where I said to her, 'It is over, we must be decisive about it.' And she wouldn't believe it, and the next two days were a screaming match, I mean quite appalling, and she tried to sleep with me, saying, 'If we get this right it is going to be all right.' I was disgusted with the whole thing by then, and I said absolutely no, and there was a terrible scene in the bedroom when she tried to make me have sex, and I wouldn't, and I had to shut myself in the bathroom in the end to get any peace. And then she did something really foul . . . she masturbated outside the door of the bathroom, and, as she came, she used the scream, the gasp of orgasm, to shout, 'I HATE YOU.' It was an act of great evil, and I remember being profoundly shocked; she used the joy and the happiness of the climax for an enormous act of hatred.

And then she became really violent, and the violence went on for two or three weeks, I mean really hitting, she smashed my glasses at one point, and she slammed a door so it cut me heavily on the face, and I was pouring blood. And I went into the bathroom and locked the door, and she stood outside, violently kicking the door, on and on and on and on, but without saying anything.

And she began taking my books and papers and burning them, she tore up the manuscript of the play I was then writing.

I rang my divorce lawyer at his home number, which he had given me for emergencies, and I said, 'There has been a lot of violence.' And he said, 'We must go for an injunction to stop her knocking you about.' So we rushed around to the law courts, found a barrister who was free, and we literally walked into a court which was empty, except for a judge sitting at the bench reading a book – he was there for just these emergencies. So the solicitor, barrister and myself sat down, and the judge looked up from his book, and my barrister said, 'My lord, in the matter of Carrington versus Carrington . . .' It was the first time I had heard those words, I hadn't thought of Carrington *versus* Carrington until then. 'Now, Mr Carrington, will you go into the witness box.' So I went into the witness box, and I went through the whole thing. The judge said, 'I will grant you an injunction for a fortnight, she mustn't knock you about, she mustn't be violent, she mustn't burn your papers and she must give you reasonable access.' So we went out, and there was the injunction in my hand: I had an injunction against my wife for violence, which was sort of unbelievable.

And then the divorce was on. And it went on for three and a half years and she fought every dirty trick in the book.

She got my professional address book, and she worked systematically through; to my knowledge she rang up seventeen of my colleagues, probably far more, and poured out every vilification, lots of stories made up, lots of appalling lies. The ones that rang me said it went in one ear and out the other, but of course there were a lot who didn't ring me, who were probably too embarrassed.

I started with a nice house in the country and a flat in London, and I finished the three and half years with no capital, a rented house, and

£80,000 worth of debts. The drama of the divorce – one could go on all day. It got to the point where the boys were having nervous breakdowns, and my hair went white in those three years.

She has remarried, she married a very rich old man in failing health, it is a very unhappy marriage. And she is vindictive beyond words towards me. She has been down to see my father twice in the nursing home, and he told me she tried to get him to cut me out of his will. She is still full of resentment.

RITA

'Don't be silly, she is just giving him a Christmas kiss . . .'

I was only 19, he was 21.

We had a lot of fun, we went out with friends all the time, in fact we spent most of our time with a crowd, which I think was one of the reasons we got married, and one of the reasons why we shouldn't have got married, I didn't see the man really, he was just someone who was fun in a crowd.

He was the first man I went to bed with. Although it was the swinging sixties, I had quite a strict upbringing, and I come from a Catholic family, and that was quite important to me – much too important, and I had a real conscience about it. It's laughable now when you look back, but that's how it was, and it tainted the relationship, and it made things tense between us, because I felt guilty.

He was Catholic too . . . and about three weeks after we slept together he asked me to marry him. We got engaged in August, and married the following July.

The year seemed to be spent saving up and planning for the wedding. I didn't admit it to anyone, but I had already realised that we weren't suited; that feeling never really left me, and, two weeks before the wedding, I really didn't want to get married, but I thought it was just a case of cold feet.

I could easily have run away. But I didn't. Duty. Catholicism. I didn't have the nerve.

The day itself was great – everyone said it was a really good wedding. We went on honeymoon, and we fought all through the honeymoon, and I don't think we ever stopped fighting. In fact the first year was one of our worst years, we fought all the time.

Actually it scarred both of us quite a lot, I think he would say the same. He didn't know how to cope with me. I used to get in a real rage and sling the dishes at him, I was highly sensitive, the least little thing would make me cry, I was in a dreadful state really. Also I had gone on the pill, which didn't suit me, I used to go down to the surgery every other week saying, 'I can't take this pill, please give me another one,' and nobody would ever believe me, because in the sixties they would never admit there was anything wrong with the pill.

As soon as I stopped taking the pill I went back to my normal self.

I had Victoria sixteen months after I had Matthew and I lost all interest in sex.

One of the main reasons was while I was in hospital having Victoria I discovered he had been seeing somebody else. I never harped on it, and I put it to the back of my mind; in the daytime you don't think about it, but at night, when you are in bed together, it's different, and I couldn't forget that he cheated on me, and he cheated on me while I was having his baby . . .

He didn't visit me very often, and before I came out, he said, 'Why don't you go to your sister's, it will do you some good.' I said, 'I don't want to go to my sister's,' but he said, 'I am going to be away up north, and I will only be worried if you don't go . . .'

Anyway, he persuaded me, and I stayed with Rosie for a few days. We were in the kitchen one morning, I think I was making a cake for her, and I heard on the news that there had been an almighty pile-up on the M1, about fifty cars were involved. And I knew he was due to drive down from Derby that morning, and I was really worried, so I phoned his company to find out if he'd got back – and *he* answered the telephone.

'Christopher?'

'No, it's not Christopher, Christopher isn't back yet . . .'

'Don't lie to me, Christopher, I know that's you.'

'I am telling you, Christopher is in Derby.'

'Christopher, I know your voice. You didn't go to Derby.'

'No, I didn't.'

So he came to my sister's that evening, and told me that he had been seeing somebody, and that he'd got me to go to my sister's so he could get me out of the way.

My brother-in-law is the most mild-mannered man, and I had

never seen him lose his temper, that is the one and only time, and he threw Christopher out and told him he was scum, and to get home and take care of his family.

I can remember the drive back: he cried all the way home, while I sat there nursing the two children. He was very apologetic, he said he didn't want to lose me, blah, blah, blah.

We never really got back to normal, nothing was ever the same . . .

And our sex life never recovered. He would make overtures to me all the time, in fact he never let up, he wasn't very understanding. I just wanted to be left alone. He would say I was frigid, he really showed no understanding in any way.

Time went on and he accepted that that's the way it was. He was always away on trips, and he got his sex elsewhere: Monday to Friday he was in hotels, so that was a good excuse to go out and find someone.

We were very short of money, he wasn't very well paid, and he was never very good with money. I remember one occasion he was away, I got a letter to say the building society was threatening to repossess our house. I was absolutely flabbergasted, I didn't even know we were behind on our mortgage. I tried to make him come home, but he said he couldn't, and I would have to cope with it.

I wasn't one for running back to my parents, and I phoned my older brother and asked him if he could loan me some money. And he phoned my mother and told her, and my parents came up to see me, and I then told them about the marriage, and that was the first they knew of any problems that we had. They were quite shocked, and they were very angry with him, told him he had to pull his socks up.

But about six months later he was seeing somebody else, and this time I asked Christopher to go – I said, 'It's finished, I can't go on any longer like this, you'd better leave.' And he was going to go, and my parents intervened again: 'Rita, remember you're a Catholic, you have two children, you must make a go of it,' and so he stayed . . .

Things changed a lot in those three years; he started running his own business, he began making a lot of money, so that was one part of the stress gone. But we still didn't have a real relationship, and we didn't discuss things, we weren't really communicating at all, we had even stopped rowing by then. Now I look back, it was better when we were rowing, because we were at least communicating. But there was nothing to say anyway. It must have been dreadful for the children.

He worked from the house and we had to run our home like a business, you could never switch off, and if the children forgot to take a message there was hell to pay. He was always at home, he'd be in the office all day, then he would work all night on his computer, business took over his life, and he had no time for the children.

But then the recession came. It started very slowly, his customers, even the large companies, one by one went down the pan, and work just dried up.

I think he went into a sort of depression, and he just couldn't cope. The failure of his business rendered him immobile for about two years, he just sat waiting for the phone to ring, but of course it didn't.

I then started to work at the local wine bar, and our total income was what I earned there. But the wine bar was an escape for me. I loved it, it was the only place I could have fun, forget about what was at home, I got on with everyone, I was able to be me, and I formed friendships which took me out of the house, and I would go out with my girlfriends and have discussions I ought to have been having with him.

At the end of the third year, we went to a Christmas party, and our hostess was very flirtatious, and she was openly flirting with Christopher. And while she was making coffee, Christopher followed her in, and I just popped my head around the door – and there they were, embracing in the kitchen. Her husband said, 'Oh, don't be silly, she is just giving him a Christmas kiss,' so I felt a bit foolish, as if I had made a fuss about nothing. But then they didn't come back for ages and I went to look for them, and they were upstairs. In bed.

I think I went into shock. I stayed in my room all the next day, and I couldn't talk to anyone, I felt suicidal. I thought: Why have I been trying to hold this marriage together, for someone who could do that to me? Although I knew he was a womaniser, I thought he had some decent instincts. Even now I still find it hard to believe, but it did happen.

So that was it, I told him we had to separate. But we couldn't afford to, he had got our finances into such a horrific state. And we tried to sell the house just as the property market slumped, and no one was buying.

He left in the end: he owed the tax people an enormous amount of money, and they came looking for him one day, and I phoned to warn him what was happening, and he didn't come home, and he hasn't been home since.

It's been hard financially, very hard. He gives me maintenance when he thinks he can afford it. I might get £80 one month, I might not get anything the next, he's barely given me half the maintenance he should have given me since he left. And I've got a mortgage on which the repayments are £900 a month – and my salary is £700 a month, and I have to maintain the children, the mortgage and our outstanding bills.

I don't make ends meet. I've started to take in lodgers, and my mother sends me food parcels. Towards the end of the month, I don't have a penny in my purse.

The marriage has dominated and wasted my life – I could have done a lot more with my life. If only we'd broken up ten years ago, when we should have done.

Most of my life is spent struggling to keep me and the children going, so there is no real time for me to feel sorry for myself.

It's nice to be able to talk to you and put some of it into perspective. But, even as I am saying things to you, I am thinking: Oh dear, why did I do that? Why did he do that? To me it's still a jumble, I still can't understand it. I don't know why he did the things he did.

What often makes me sad is that my sister and her husband have got a wonderful relationship, and my parents were the same, but they were very romantic. Often I think I've never had that, and I don't think I will, with the situation I am in, I've just got that feeling . . .

MARCIA

Chris was just super-macho, he wore cowboy boots in hundred-degree weather because he felt sneakers were faggy-looking . . .

We were in a Bertolt Brecht play called *The Resistable Rise of Arturo Ui* which is about a bunch of gangsters, and I was the gun moll; actually, he had a really small part in the play and I had a really big part, and I didn't pay much attention to him. I had a scene where I had to be sewing one of the guy's garments, and in rehearsal I didn't have anything to sew so Chris lent me his leather jacket, and, while I was sewing it, a switch blade fell out on to the floor, and that's what made me fall in love with him.

I thought that was very glamorous and different, and I looked at him with new eyes, and we then started talking. The run of this play was about three or four months and over the course of that time I started getting increasingly attracted to him.

Chris was dealing coke on a very serious level, I mean Colombian guys with guns would be waiting outside the rehearsal halls, and he would be talking to them in Spanish and running here and there and sweating; Chris spoke Spanish fluently, he had run away from home when he was 17 and hung out on the streets of New York and learnt Colombian-accented Spanish from these guys.

Chris was just super-macho, he wore cowboy boots in hundred-degree weather because he felt sneakers were faggy-looking, he was very skinny, coke-dealer skinny, tight black jeans, leather jacket, sun glasses all the time – and I allowed myself to live out the fantasy of being a beautiful woman on a tough guy's arm. It was the most glamorous I ever felt in my life, and as I rode around on the back of his motor cycle I felt very sexy.

It was wonderful the first summer we were in New York together, very romantic, and I felt super-cool and hip to be his woman; we'd go out to dinner and I wouldn't wear any underwear, and we would be walking down the streets on the 4th of July, high, and sweating, with fireworks going off all over, and it felt very right. But there was a lot of coke in the whole picture, Chris did drugs twenty-four hours a day, he was freebasing on coke very heavily, and he smoked pot continuously, he would smoke pot the way other people would smoke cigarettes: so, looking back, it wasn't wonderful at all, it was really a mess.

I was still going on my auditions and doing everything normal in my life; the only thing was that I got offered a lot of work and turned it all down because I wanted to be with him.

Then he directed a play he had written which I thought was a piece of shit, very juvenile humour, not at all funny, and bad musical numbers, and when I told him my opinion he got really angry, and that became our first bone of contention.

We fought a lot during that time. But in February I went to Kentucky to do a play, and while I was away I thought of our relationship as being very romantic, and I was in love again, and when I got back he gave me diamond earrings and asked me to marry him, and I said yes.

Everything was pretty good for that first year. I got a really high-paying job on a soap opera with the most money I have ever made in my life, so we were living great. I got pregnant twice and had two abortions, but that was because I was working, and also Chris absolutely did not want children.

The abortions changed everything for me, and not having sex changed everything for him; it wasn't that we weren't having sex, it was just that I didn't have the total abandon about it. I had a lot of pain, I was scared, and we never dealt with that, it was all pushed under. What happened really was that we drifted apart, because our strongest bond was the sexual thing, it was all we really had that was mutual, and once that was gone I just became this weepy, frightened, childlike person, and he couldn't deal with that at all.

I made him give up his drug business and because I was making a lot of money I said I would buy his coke. I was scared that I was going to get into a lot of trouble: his business was too obvious – all these drug runners coming to the door, and I knew we would get caught and I would get arrested and my face would be in the *New York Post.*

And that was the end, asking him to give up dealing was like cutting his balls off, he said, and we never stopped fighting over that.

However, he agreed to give up dealing and then he became financially dependent on me, which was no problem when I was making a fortune, but I never wanted to be a soap opera actress, and after a while I quit the series to do a play which paid nothing. And he hit the roof, he couldn't believe I wouldn't want that money. He really resented me when he had to get a job. He got a job tending a bar on 8th Street called the B-Bop which I don't think is there any more.

He then started getting scary. He gained a lot of weight and became really built up, and got into kick boxing and started carrying guns, and he began getting physically violent and was angry with me all the time.

As soon as I could afford to, I moved out. He would call me up and cry on the telephone endlessly: 'I need you, I want you to come home,' and, 'I love you so much.' And then I'd come back, and he would just be so mean to me, not letting me in the door, and I would have to go through a scene begging to come in, and saying I was sorry. More than once he had me on the floor, with his hand around my neck and a butcher's knife pointed at my neck.

I went to Houston to do a play and I fell in love with somebody there, and I called Chris up on the phone and told him it was absolutely, definitely over between us, although the other man was married, so that wasn't very healthy either . . .

DAVID

I pleaded to get back together again, I didn't want the marriage to end – being found out suddenly brought me to my senses . . .

I first caught sight of Rosie in a restaurant on the other side of the room: she was celebrating her 21st birthday party. I didn't know who she was, but I said to the waiter, 'She's very pretty,' and to my embarrassment he went over and said, 'The gentleman over there thinks you're lovely,' and I got a message back saying, 'Well, I think he's very nice too.' I got her telephone number, and rang her the following day.

On the first date I asked her to marry me. I said, 'I always wanted an E-type Jaguar and I've got that, and I want you and I'm going to have you . . .'

She said, 'You always get what you want, do you?' And I said yes I did, and about a year later we did get married, and we had our son a year after that.

Everything was fine until we moved from London to a village in Oxfordshire – that's when it all started going wrong really. We got to know quite a few showbusiness people who lived around there, and this particular woman fancied me, and I quite fancied her as well, to be honest, and my relationship with this lady got rather closer than it should have done, and we had an affair.

It got to a stage where I was taking ridiculous risks, ringing her up when my wife was in the house; it was stupid, we were being blatantly obvious about it, I mean at parties we used to disappear down the end of the garden, things like that.

But I really enjoyed it, and I needed it, because I got affection from her that I wasn't getting at home. Sexually, Rosie and I weren't compatible, there was lack of affection, particularly on her part. I like making love, but I didn't get the feeling she enjoyed it; if I'm out on the streets, I like to hold hands, but she never liked that, she wasn't tactile. It was all rather cold, and I actually got to the stage where I felt lonely in my own home.

I think probably we weren't made for one another really, it's as simple as that. I fell in love with somebody who was pretty to look at, but there wasn't enough between us.

I was doing very well at the time, I was doing television as well as pursuing my film career, and she started not getting work. In a way I was quite glad she wasn't working, because I am very jealous. If she had gone to work, I would think she might do what I was doing, exchanging telephone numbers and being a bit of an old tart.

And then I got found out. She accused me of having an affair, which I denied, so she didn't pursue that, but she knew I had, and she said she wasn't in love with me any more. I realised that I'd messed up, and I wanted to try and get back together again. And she didn't want to.

I pleaded to get back together again, I didn't want the marriage to end – being found out suddenly brought me to my senses. I wanted her to stay with me, I wanted to get things right, I was still in love with her, but she wasn't in love with me, and unfortunately you can't force somebody to love you.

I pleaded with her not to go, I became desperate, but there was nothing I could do about it, and, while I was filming at the studio, she moved out, and when I came back there was nothing there, that was it . . .

I remember, when I got home, I went into my son's room, and all his stuff had gone . . . he'd gone. I went into our room, and all her stuff had gone . . . it was just a dead house. And then I broke down and cried.

It was such a dreadful thing to happen, my life had gone, my life with her had gone, and I was terribly ashamed of letting my son down.

I would collect my son almost every weekend, but it was upsetting seeing him and then taking him back – I used to go home and cry my eyes out.

I just wanted to get her back again. I was always trying to get her to come back.

At one stage I think there was a chance we might have got back together again. We went out to dinner, we went to a restaurant in

Oxford, an Italian restaurant. We were getting along well, and I said, 'Why don't you just come back and try it, you can still keep your house, or I could move in with you . . .' and there was a chance it might have worked, and somebody tipped off Fleet Street that we were out together, and it appeared in a gossip column the following day. And she accused me of setting it up, of doing a publicity job, and that completely ruined things, that one incident actually stopped us getting back together again.

How could she think I'd tipped the paper off? I hadn't, genuinely, on my honour, I hadn't, it must have been the waiter. And that really did put the nail in the coffin.

Losing her brought home to me how much I loved her, I was still very much in love with her, and it took me a good six years to get over her.

I became very nervy, and my doctor put me on valium. And I actually got addicted to valium, and I started drinking too much. At one stage I was taking so much valium I nearly got knocked over walking out in front of a car; at night I had to take a lot of valium to get to sleep, and I was also taking some stuff called Tuinal, a barbiturate. It didn't do my career very much good, I talked too much about it, I talked about it on the air, I talked to the newspapers, and I got criticised a great deal for doing that.

After a time she married someone else, and I had to go through the process of taking my son back to their family unit, and then going home to an empty house, and I started feeling pretty sorry for myself. I still made attempts to get her back. But she wasn't interested, she just wasn't interested. And I then realised there was no chance. Her new marriage is very stable, and they'll be together for ever.

I didn't go out with anybody for a good few years after that. I then found it very strange asking somebody out, picking them up, having to get an *A–Z* to find out where they live; it was like going back to being a teenager again.

But I was still in love with Rosie, and when I went out on these dates I tended to talk about my marriage – I eventually worked out why it was that nobody wanted to go out with me a second time!

The strange thing is, I can hardly remember being married to her now; I can remember certain things, I remember coming home from work and cutting the grass, and she was watching me with Timmy tucked under her arm. I remember going to Fiji on our honeymoon, and I remember being in bed with her one night, pleading with her not to leave me. Apart from that, I don't remember anything.

I wouldn't want to be married to her again, that feeling left me quite a long time ago. I now see her as a friend, just a friend, and if I didn't see her again it wouldn't bother me in the slightest.

But I'm certainly glad I got married to her, for my son, because he's a great joy to me, I love him immensely, and the joy that I've had from him is immeasurable.

Now I've met someone amazing, and I'm very happy. This is something that's only been going on for a few months, but I know it will go on for a long, long time. But the last fourteen years I have been through dreadful loneliness, and I did go through deep despair. I came out of that after the age of 40, when I came to terms with the fact that life isn't perfect.

ZOË

I had friends who had joined dating agencies, and they seemed to have had a good time, and so I thought I would do that . . .

Eighteen months ago the man that I had been living with was killed. Jonathan was killed on a motor bike. We had been living together for five years, and life was going to go on with us for ever; we had just bought a house together, we were planning to get married, and we had been very happy. So I was a bit distraught, in fact I know now that I am still grieving him an awful lot.

Friends and family were brilliant, they did everything that they could do, but they can't go through the grieving for you.

The difficulty was that I had just started a business, and I had got twelve people in my company, and I had to keep going, the survival of the business depended on me keeping going. And in many respects I think that was a mistake, I should have stopped work for a month or something, and tried to come to terms with his death. But I didn't, my response was that I wanted to find somebody and carry on my life where I had left off with Jonathan, I wanted to replace him. I just felt so lost, so alone in my sadness, and I think my grief had eroded all my confidence. I just wanted to be happy again, that was all.

I did a bit of dating, but I just couldn't get into the swing of it, and then last summer I felt really quite good about myself, and felt that I was ready to start looking for a proper relationship.

I had friends who had joined dating agencies, and they seemed to have had a good time, and so I thought I would do that.

I went along to the agency, and I liked the girl who met me there. Well, they screen you very thoroughly: they do a financial search, you have to take a medical test, they examine a handwriting analysis, and you see a psychologist who does a report on you. And then they say we think you would probably like to meet *this* person, and they tell you about him, and show you his dossier.

And if you say yes, I think I might like to meet him, they do the same with him, and, if all's well, the chap rings the girl up, it's always that way, and if you get on over the phone, then you arrange to meet – and then it's up to the two of you.

Keith rang me at the office. He is a very bright, intelligent, interesting man, a Cambridge graduate. The thing that appealed to me about him was that he was widely read, he seemed to be very in touch with himself, he could chat for a long time, and I enjoyed talking to him.

The next step was to arrange to meet, and we set a date in our diaries for about a week from that time of speaking. And then, on the day, he rang me up and said, 'Meet me at Battersea heliport at 5 o'clock,' and put the phone down. And I thought: Battersea heliport, I wonder if he is getting a shuttle or something. But it turned out that he had his own helicopter, which was rather dynamic. We went for a drink, and then for dinner. His passion is business, and I am a businesswoman, so I could talk at great length to him about lots of things, and we got on really well. And after dinner, we went to his sister's house in Fulham, and I really warmed to him then because, when we walked into her house, she was obviously so thrilled to see him, and they were so close, very warm and affectionate with one another, and seeing them together completely at ease – that was the clincher, and I just thought: God, this man is really loving and giving and intelligent.

And so basically the evening couldn't have gone better.

I went home that night, and I was really looking forward to the prospect of seeing him again, but he was supposed to be going away to the States for a holiday at the weekend, and it was my birthday that weekend, so that was a disappointment, but nothing major, it was early days. He rang the next day, and we chatted a long time, and then he rang me again at the end of the week and said, 'I am not going away now, how about if we meet over the weekend?' I was thrilled. He said there was a charity ball and various other things we could do: why didn't I come up to him for the weekend. And I thought that was a great idea, so I hopped on a train, and he met me, he has a lovely house in Suffolk, and we spent the day together, and he proposed to me that night, he proposed to me outside the house on a beautiful, star-spangled evening.

Actually, he had been building up to it all evening in various ways. He had said, 'If I was to ask you to marry me, would you say yes?' And I said, 'That sounds rather like a proposal to me,' and he said, 'Well, I guess it is.' And I told him, 'I don't think now is the time to say something like that, you have had a lot to drink . . .' so I didn't take it seriously, were it not for the fact that he was most insistent the next morning.

And in the morning nothing had changed. In fact it became even more romantic as time went on, it escalated into the impossible, I suppose.

That Sunday we had breakfast out on the terrace, and it was a beautiful summer's day, warm, clear blue skies, and he wanted to talk about the proposal again. He was really insistent – and I was bowled over. And so it was yes.

And then he wanted to talk about the arrangements and when we were going to do it: he wanted to do it at the end of the week, but I managed to persuade him that we should wait a little bit longer. I didn't tell my family right away, I still couldn't quite believe it, so I left it for a day – and then I realised that it really was real, and I wanted to continue with it. And so I never left. I arrived for that weekend, and we got married two weeks later.

Everyone was thrilled, they just thought this was the best thing, even though it was a bit wild: because I had had such a terrible time before, I think they thought: Hurray, she is going to be really happy now.

Well, his business was very hard work at that point, so we could only snatch a night away, but we went to a nice country hotel, and we had a wonderful time then, absolutely wonderful, and we were very open and communicative and close, and that continued, and gained momentum.

I started working with him; he was under enormous pressure, and it was agreed that I could positively contribute. And we used to do things like go off to Paris for the weekend, part business and part pleasure. We travelled around a great deal, we just seemed to do an awful lot together. And it was great, it was really great for a very short period of time, and the culmination of that was the point where Keith said to me, 'This is just the most beautiful experience I have ever had

– I never thought I would be able to love anybody like this, and I can't imagine life without you.'

Almost the next day there was a complete change in him. This is only my assessment of it: he equates loving somebody with something really ghastly, and OK, he had married me, but as soon as he'd gone the whole length in his loving me, he was absolutely terrified.

He started not to talk to me, so we would have long periods of deathly silence. He was very depressed. Before we got married, he had said, 'I can get grumpy,' but what he didn't tell me was that he actually gets severely depressed, and very stressed: he used to wake up in the morning and throw up. I managed to bolster him up a few times, and we would go through peaks and troughs, but more and more I was losing myself, being swallowed up by the emotional trauma of it.

I tried really hard to laugh and be positive, because I am a pretty bubbly sort of person, but I think he liked to undermine me; if I was feeling happy he would make me feel as though I had no right to be, and if I felt sad it was because I wasn't capable of coping with the situation. It was very unreasonable.

The physical contact on a day to day basis and the caring for one another totally dried up, although I tried, because if I am there I am going to be trying. But there would be no eye contact, no touching, in fact he would blatantly ignore me. He reduced me to two inches high.

In the context of the relationship I knew everything was lost, and it felt incredibly lonely.

We did talk about it, I forced a conversation, but he was only prepared to say that it was my fault, and, if I was prepared to acknowledge that, then there was a discussion point. If he had to bear some responsibility for it, he didn't want to know.

At Christmas we were meant to go away with some very close friends of mine, and I just couldn't bear to put up a front of being the happy, newly wedded wife; I knew I would crumble, and that would distress them terribly. So I said to him,'I must go away without you, and we will have to see what happens.' And I rang him on New Year, and I said, 'We can really make this work,' and he said, 'I don't want to, I don't want to be married.' And I said, 'You are saying you want a divorce,' and he said, 'Yes, that's what I want.' And I rang him again the next day, and he was insistent, so I went back and packed a few belongings, and came down to London, and stayed with my brother.

In fact when I went to his house for the last time, he was really strangely caring, no, not caring, affectionate, which is different: he didn't want to know where I was going to live, or whether I was going to be all right, but he was sort of pleased to see me, and I think relieved that I had made my mind up there wasn't going to be any angry exchange of words. I felt enormous sadness.

I've seen him a few times since then – we have managed to get some form of communication going which I feel happy about. I don't think about him very much now, I guess it was a brief enough time – although very traumatic. I don't feel any malice towards him, I feel quite sorry for him because I think he will do it again.

But now I am into building my future, and I have learnt that my happiness and my well-being don't depend on somebody else, they depend on me.

If I had known that before, if I hadn't been so keen to try and replace what I had lost, I don't think I would have ever married him.

GLYNIS

I had to be shown what to do, you *have to lie down, and this is how things happen . . . and I remember thinking that it was rather messy . . .*

I met him through my brother; they had just come home from Hong Kong, and they had been out together on a riotous night in their uniforms, and my brother had lost his cap. It turned out that he had another cap at home, and so when he and Richard came to the house, I was introduced to him.

I was 16, very much the kid sister, and I was very young mentally as well as physically. Richard was about twelve years older than me.

Being a friend of my brother's, I accepted him, and he began to come around from time to time. He invited me to the cinema, and we started courtship.

I remember, after a few times of going out, he tried to kiss me goodnight – I always shook hands goodnight. And, as he tried to kiss me, I stood with very clenched lips, never having kissed anyone in my life, and he said, 'I am not one of your schoolfriends, you know.' Subsequently I thought: Well, how do you kiss? But I can't pretend I was terribly curious. I was too young to think what we were doing – Richard was just someone I went to the cinema and dancing with.

I don't know why we got married. I think that at times he reminded me of my father – there were certain mannerisms, certain angles of his head that reminded me of my father – and I'd been very fond indeed of my father, and I think that's about as far as I got in my calculations.

Then things escalated because my stepfather, who was in the RAF, was being posted, and I had decided that I wouldn't go with them. I was going to take a bed-sitting room with a local couple, and go in for nursing. And then the subject of marriage came up, and we got married, it was as simple as that.

I truthfully do not remember how it happened; when I look back on it now, I wasn't thinking at all about what I was doing. I was much too immature to be making decisions like that.

We married on the day of my stepfather's posting. We got married in the morning, and they went off on the train in the afternoon, and we moved straight in with my parents-in-law.

We hadn't slept together before the wedding. Sex didn't really mean much to me one way or the other, and I suppose you could say, to put it in a rather corny way, I was not awakened by him, and I never enjoyed the sexual side of it, I had to be shown what to do, *you* have to lie down, and this is how things happen . . . and I remember thinking that it was rather messy.

Also, it was quite difficult because we were in a relatively small house, with a very prying father-in-law, and I was very self-conscious and so was my husband; it was very important to have privacy, we needed privacy, and I remember my father-in-law complaining because we were talking too loudly, and this was disturbing the house.

I don't think the marriage worked from the word go. This man would go off to his rugby matches, and go to the rugby club, and he continued his social life much as he had been doing: nothing changed for him. He would still go dancing, he would play cards until the early hours, while I always stayed at home. He was the original double-standards man.

My life was going to work, coming home, spending time with a much adored mother-in-law, and an extremely difficult father-in-law, and I wasn't thinking outside that; I was programmed to do what I was told, I was like a child really. He was my husband, and you did as your husband expected you to do – where I got this idea from I don't know.

It took me a little time to catch on to what was happening to me, and I remember going to the local doctor, and him saying, 'You are expecting a child.' When I started to show my pregnancy, my husband said that he found it embarrassing to be seen with me, and after that I don't think we ever once went out together.

And then my father-in-law made a pass at me, and I was terrified that this would be discovered either by my husband or my mother-in-law. He came up behind me one day, and put his arms around my waist, and, as I froze, he moved his arms upwards so his hands were on my breasts, and I was afraid to be alone with him after that.

I went looking for a house, and I found a cottage, and, with my sister and a friend of hers, we did this cottage up, we decorated it and got it ready. My husband said he wouldn't see the cottage until after it had been decorated, because 'it might spoil it for him', and he saw it for the first time on the day that my sister and I moved everything in. He walked around and said it looked quite nice, and that was the end of the comment. He still went out that evening.

There was no telephone in the cottage – the public telephone was about fifteen minutes away, and my concern was how was I going to phone for the local nurse, because this second child was going to be born in the cottage, and leave the baby unattended. And I said to my husband, 'You should be here, at least until after the baby is born,' and his reaction was: 'It's typical of you to be so selfish. Has it not occurred to you that I may not want to be there when the baby is born – men don't like that kind of thing.'

It got to the stage where I just couldn't sleep with him; he was quite forceful for a while, and, if he was forceful, I gave in. My second tactic was to pretend to be asleep when he got back in the early hours, although normally he would wake me.

It was a marriage that couldn't have worked and it didn't work from day one. Nothing could have made that marriage work. I tried to discuss the marriage with him, but to no avail. I used to ask him to stay in, I remember once or twice really pleading with him.

I must by this time have been deeply depressed, and I remember crying rivers alone in my room. And I was beginning to find it difficult to speak to people. I remember getting to a stage where, if I saw someone I knew, I would cross the street. And because I didn't know what to do with myself, I would go to bed when the children went to bed, even if that was six o'clock.

And then I decided, for him to treat me like this, there must be something wrong with *me*, so I spoke to my doctor, and I said, 'I think I have to see a psychiatrist,' not knowing the least bit what they were. I remember the psychiatrist saying, 'But there is nothing wrong with you – now send your husband to me, and we might get somewhere.' Richard was outraged, he said, 'Do you know the shame it would bring on me if my friends discovered that my wife had been to a psychiatrist?' End of story.

I was 21 when I left. It was getting to the stage where the rows and the atmosphere in the house were beginning to affect my eldest child, and I was also afraid that, if I stayed, I was just going to go on getting pregnant, whether I liked it or not.

I went to stay with my mother and stepfather, I was so exhausted, I could hardly move. And after a few days, I said to my mother, 'I can't go back.' 'Darling,' she said, 'what's the matter?' By this time I was practically inarticulate, and I couldn't or wouldn't give any further explanation. I would say nothing, except, 'I can't go back.'

I remember my parents took me out to dinner, and I was in such a state I couldn't hold the knife and fork properly, and they kept dropping on the floor. I suppose I was so depressed by this time I could barely co-ordinate.

He wrote me very romantic letters when I was away. He wrote me one which said, 'You are not coming back, are you?' And then he rang me, and he said, 'I will kill myself.' And I remember saying, 'I don't care what you do, I am not coming back,' feeling absolutely nothing. And there was a record out by Jim Reeves, it was 'Put Your Sweet Lips a Little Closer to the Phone', and he said, 'Do listen to that record,' and I remember thinking: Absolutely not. It was too late, I wasn't going back.

But I got better. You see, you fight for your children, you'll do things for your children that you won't do for yourself, and I got a very small place quite close to my parents, and we moved in there.

I subsequently formed a relationship with a man who died not so many years ago now. We were together for over twenty years. I would not marry him, although he wanted to get married very much, and I certainly regarded it as a marriage, but I didn't want the relationship contaminated by what had been my experience of marriage. I loved this man very much, and he loved me, he was wonderful from start to finish. I had no reason to fear marrying him, but the scar of that experience was so deep I just didn't want to.

He had a terrific sense of humour, he was extremely perceptive, he was extraordinarily kind, and he was bold in a gentle way. He was able to overcome all of the hangups that I had by this time, but he did it gently, very lovingly.

I remember the glow of making the transition from hopelessness to happiness once he was romantically in my life; I can remember the feeling of security and the total lack of fear, and I can remember thinking: This man laughs such a lot. He was a wonderful man . . .

My ex-husband must be in his early-60s now, and I have no curiosity about him whatsoever. If there had not been children I probably would have forgotten him completely a long time ago. I think I have forgiven him, but I can't forgive him on my children's behalf, you understand, although they are adults now. He has not seen them since I left.

There was no way we could have made the marriage work: I think we did each other an equal disservice by getting married in the first place.

ANGIE

He . . . kicked me in the chest . . . and threw me across the hallway. I was on the floor and he ripped my wedding ring off and began trying to ram it down my throat . . . he was just demonic. I don't know how he didn't kill me, I was expecting him to . . .

Well, he was working at the same police station. He was devastatingly handsome, very blond, very tall, he was very aloof with people, men as well. We went to a party one evening and he gave me a lift home.

He came in and we just sat and talked until about four o'clock in the morning, and when he left he didn't kiss me goodbye or anything. I can remember thinking how nice not fighting somebody off just because you've invited them in for coffee.

And then he asked me out again, and again he brought me back and left without giving me a kiss, and this went on for quite a few weeks, and I started thinking: This is really weird.

We went out one night to a party and when we got back there was somebody asleep in a car at the bottom of the road, and I said, 'That's an odd place for somebody to sleep,' and he said, 'Well, if he's still there in the morning I'll check him out.' So I assumed from that he was going to stay the night, which he did. And I honestly can't remember anything about that, so it couldn't have been that mind-blowing.

I could only have known him a few months before he moved in; I had already decided by then I was going to marry him, and when he proposed I was absolutely thrilled to bits.

But as soon as we got engaged he used to say I didn't dress the right way, he didn't like me smoking, he didn't like the fact that I bit my nails, and he used to berate me for being fat – I was a lot heavier than I am now.

Eight weeks before we got married we had a huge row and I

thought: I can't marry him, I just can't marry him, but the invitations had gone out, my frock had been made, and I kept thinking this must be pre-wedding nerves.

On the way to the church, I can remember Dad saying,'You're really sure you want to do this?' And I said, 'Yes, yes, I'm sure,' but I wasn't at all.

I didn't want to leave the reception, I wanted to stay with all my friends, I certainly didn't want to be with him. Dad had booked us four nights at the Hilton as a wedding present, and we didn't say a word to each other in the car going up to London.

When we got to our room there was a bottle of champagne, which he proceeded to drink, and he immediately fell asleep. I thought: Well, that often happens on someone's wedding night. But in the morning I can remember waking up and opening my eyes, seeing my hand on the pillow with the wedding ring, and my heart just sinking, realising I hadn't dreamt it, I'd really done it.

I was desperate for a cigarette – I used to smoke secretly because he thought I'd given up, and I kept wishing he'd go out so I could have a fag. We went to bed that night and again he made no effort; he didn't kiss me or touch me all the time we were there.

It rained a lot, it rained an awful lot, and the only thing I can really remember about my honeymoon was hearing on the radio that Yvonne Fletcher got shot outside the Iranian Embassy.

It hadn't been mad passionate sex before we got married, three or four times a week, but it literally stopped as soon as we got married. In fact, moving forward, it was actually five months before we did it again.

The subject of sex was dynamite, I mean it was like touching a live fuse whenever I mentioned it. I would ask, 'Is it me, is there something wrong with me?'

'No, no, I'm just tired . . . I can't just turn myself on and off at the switch of a button.' I used to read books on how to seduce your man, and I can remember one night getting into bed with him, and I put my hand where I thought he would find it exciting, and he looked at me and said, 'What are you doing?' I felt humiliated, and I quickly took my hand away, and he said, 'I'm going downstairs to get a drink.' I started thinking: Well, obviously it's me, there's something wrong with me.

Twelve weeks after we were married, he was late turn, so he should have been home at ten-thirty. He turned up at two-thirty in the morning, paralytic.

I said, 'Where have you been?' And he just punched me straight in the middle of my face, and then slapped me around the head. I went upstairs to bed not believing what had happened. I'd spent so many years in my job going to domestic situations and sorting them out, and suddenly here was the man I'd married, and he'd just broken my nose – which was what he did.

The next day I asked him, 'Are you sorry you did it?' And he said, 'No, you bloody deserved it.'

At that point I should have ended this marriage, but I thought: I've only been married twelve weeks, he won't do it again. Experience should have kicked me up the arse and said: Oh yes he will, because I knew, from the number of times I used to go back to the same addresses to deal with the same people, that men don't hit a woman just once. And that was the beginning of him knocking me about.

I've been in very violent situations at work, I was at the Brixton riots and the Southall riots, but that was always different because it wasn't aimed at me personally, it was me the police officer. With him it was me, and I found that very hard to deal with.

The problem was that there was nobody I could tell. Because of our job I knew how I'd be looked at if I reported my husband for hitting me; so I was going to work with a black eye, saying, 'Oh, I walked into the door knocker,' you know, those dumb excuses you always expect people to believe . . . and they know you're telling lies. Of course eventually he hit me in places where people wouldn't see, and left my face alone.

I tried to get him to find me attractive. I made three or four advances to him, I even got him really drunk one night, because I thought: Maybe if we do it once he'll get to like it again. In the end I just stopped trying.

I can remember him saying to me one night, 'How can you expect me to find you attractive when you lay there like a great lump of white pork?' He used to tell me how fat I was and how ugly I looked, how no man could ever find me attractive. And in the end I actually believed everything he was saying to me, and my opinion of myself was rock bottom.

I can't remember now why on earth we did it five months later, but it was just horrible. We never had sex again.

He initiated it. There was no love there, it was: I'll jump on top of you and screw you, and then turn over and go to sleep. And that was it, he left me laying there thinking: Well, Jesus, if this is what I've been waiting for for five months, why did I bother?

And that's when I conceived Lucy. I had no intentions of having a child, but I had a cap in the bathroom – which I used to think had perished through lack of use – and I can remember thinking: Christ, I can't get up and get it because by the time I've done that he'll have gone off the idea.

He was just so unkind to me while I was pregnant. And when she was about two months old things got worse. He was drinking a lot, and he used to do things like smash bottles and jab the glass towards my face to see me flinch. And always this verbal stuff, just running me down and saying how disgusting a person I was. He really really hated me. I couldn't understand what it was I'd done wrong, I kept saying to him, 'Tell me what I've done, just tell me what I've done wrong.'

My kidney packed up and I had to go into hospital, and, while I was there, he actually came in to see me. He said he'd been out for a drink with his friend Dennis the night before, and he said he stayed the night. I said, 'What, in our house? Where did he sleep?' And Simon said, 'In our bed.' So I said, 'Well, where did you sleep?' And Simon said, 'In our bed.'

I was a bit drowsy because I'd had an anaesthetic. And I can remember saying, 'Well, are you AC/DC, or what?' And he just shrugged his shoulders. And it finally clicked that I had married somebody who was homosexual; it took all that time for it to finally slot into place.

It was like a dawning for me, and I can remember thinking: Well, that's what it was . . . And then it was my big quest to get him to admit he was homosexual, because it would almost have exonerated me, I could have thought: Well, it wasn't me, it was because I wasn't a man. But he would never admit it.

I came out of hospital and he went to live with Dennis, and I'd get Dennis phoning me up in tears saying, 'He's just hit me and we've had this awful row.' And I was saying, 'Dennis, don't bloody ring *me* up.'

After Christmas Dennis and he split up, and Simon came back here late one night. I can remember him coming through the front door, he was drunk, very very drunk, and I took one look at him and thought: Jesus, this is going to be it again.

And he started doing this Kung Fu stuff, he made a flying jump at me and kicked me in the chest, and I turned around to walk away and he grabbed a handful of my hair and threw me across the hallway. I was on the floor and he ripped my wedding ring off and began trying to ram it down my throat, and he was saying, 'I'm going to kill you, I'm going to kill you,' he was just demonic. I don't know how he didn't kill me, I was expecting him to.

That was it then – I've not seen or heard from him since that night.

I didn't tell anyone in the police force he was homosexual for a long time. I wasn't proud of the fact I'd made this huge cock-up and married someone who was gay; if I worked in a different environment with different people it wouldn't have been a problem, but the job I was in, it was enormously difficult, so many policemen find them disgusting and abhorrent.

If I hadn't got pregnant when I did, I would have got the hell out. I'd never be without her now, but it's not been easy because she is his child, she has his blond hair, she has his look on her face. I just thank God she wasn't a boy.

PAUL

By and large, we had a happy marriage . . . despite lacking romance and love and affection . . .

I met my first wife when I went to work in Paris as a student hotelier. She was working in the flower shop, and I thought she was quite attractive, and started to date her. She was French, and the prospect of learning a language at the same time as getting laid was quite a pleasant one.

I was only there for six months, and we had a nice time together; it wasn't intended that it should go on, I was going to go back to England. As it happened she became pregnant, which I only found out about when she wrote to me. I then had choices to make. I felt the world rather a large, daunting place at the age of 20, I was a little bit frightened of it, but I felt I could probably be a bit stronger if I had someone to lean on. And here was a person who would make a very fine wife, very nice, good-natured, so I felt that maybe this was the right person, and I should grab it by both hands and get married, and that is exactly what I did.

It went very well. In total I was married sixteen years, and the first ten years were brilliant, they suited me down to the ground. I need something to work for, and immediately having three children indeed gave me something to work for, and, although I am a ladies' man, the first ten years I was completely faithful, and my happiness was derived from working for my family.

I literally didn't have more than £50 in my pocket when I got married, and we managed to buy a very substantial house in Epsom and drive super BMW cars, and so the rewards of my hard work were living a very good lifestyle. The secret to this and to all life is to be progressive; life has to be ongoing, there's got to be growth.

Mireille contributed a lot to this. She was not only a good mother, but she worked jolly hard, and the whole thing flew along. And then, rightly or wrongly, I bought her a business, and this actually became her persona: she felt that she was lacking in character, therefore she took on the character of the business, which was a couture shop. She took on 'the overdraft', and all I had were years of her grumbling about it. I said, 'If you don't like it, sell it, you don't need it,' and she would never have that. So it became her life, and she became the job. It's seven years since I left home, and she is still the same.

I would get home before my wife and start to cook for the children, which I didn't mind doing, but then I could look forward to this grumpy individual coming home at 7.30–8.00 p.m., with, 'Oh, the overdraft.' And I got fed up with it, and year after year I longed to be free of this stagnant situation: it wasn't growing, and whatever I am involved with has to be forward-moving.

We had very different working hours. I would finish working at two or three in the morning, and she had to get up at six to get the children to school, so sexually you feel a bit bad to have to go home and wake your wife up because you are feeling randy. So you look for these kind of things elsewhere . . .

There were cheeky little bits of goings on, little flings, and they were fun and exciting and served a purpose: they took away the sexual pressure I needed to get rid of.

The first woman I saw on a regular basis was great fun; I used to see her every Thursday, which was her day off. I called her my funny fuck, because I used to laugh when I was there. It wasn't particularly enjoyable sex, in fact it was only with her I put the television on at the same time, but she wasn't demanding, she didn't ask for anything at all. I think she enjoyed the fact I was successful, and she was a good way down the pecking line, and, as is very often the case with women, liked to have an affair with the man at the top, and I was exciting and interesting to her.

I continued to live with my wife, but I obviously no longer gave my affections to her – even if you are not in love with the girl you are having a fling with, you cannot keep running back and loving your wife. You might have a bit now and again on the side, and maintain a loving relationship with your wife, but if you are going to have regular bits on the side, then there is something fundamentally wrong with your marriage. And something was fundamentally wrong with our marriage.

But by and large, we had a happy marriage, we didn't argue, we didn't row, we were kind to each other, and despite lacking romance and love and affection I never believed that it was a bad situation.

But I had to leave. The most difficult thing is to actually initiate that kind of conversation, and I think it is very brave people or weird people that can actually do it. Usually it's only after something's happened that you actually sit down and are able to communicate, and often people will deliberately be found out in order to be able to broach the subject.

There were periods when I had more flings than others, but then there was somebody I actually fell in love with. I've been in love in my life six times altogether, all very different and very interesting, but the last occasion was a girl my wife knew, Joanna, who in fact was a very good friend of hers.

I got very involved with her, and she was the little bit of help I needed to leave. I needed to be free. I used to live day by day before I got married, and I'd lost that. I was part of this group who is going to have annual holidays, new carpets, new fridges, retirement, death . . . and I felt: I have got to get out of it.

But before I could have the talk, I contracted nonspecific urethritis, you're peeing, and it burns – I am probably lucky I didn't catch anything else during those years. And I then had to tell my wife, because, although it is not a very serious disease, it's sexually transmittable – and I used that as the moment to say well, I think we should have a break, and she agreed, and I moved out then.

I can be undecided on many issues, but, if I make my mind up, that's it, and having decided to leave home and turn my back on them I had no doubts.

I was very happy living with Joanna. And yet, after three months, I saw my wife was unhappy, and she was to my mind starting to go a bit potty: she had me followed, she followed me herself, she broke down terribly. And I suddenly said to myself: Whether it's making me happy or not, I just can't do it to this woman, and I decided to go back, for my wife's health.

As soon as I put my foot over the threshold, I knew I was doing the wrong thing, and I knew that was not where I wanted to be. It was very embarrassing and awkward: I couldn't bear my wife to touch me.

I was in the kitchen on the first day, and my wife put her hand on my shoulder – and I jumped through the roof. And I couldn't sleep with her. I said, 'Look, it's going to take some time for us to settle down,' I made that as an excuse, and I slept in the spare room. I stayed a week, and at the end of the week, we both knew it was not going to work, so off I went, and within a year we were divorced.

I kept the identity of the woman I was living with secret because I think Mireille would have been upset to find out who it was, and she would have made the divorce awkward. I did tell her after the divorce.

The divorce was very easy for me – I think my wife was divorced before she actually realised it.

Immediately she sought solace in a much older man, who was obviously not going to run away from her. And they bought a house together, and she left the children to live with this guy: the kids were then 16 and 17. It was very unfortunate – I couldn't say anything really because I had done the same thing, but the kids must have thought: What's wrong with us? First father leaves home, and then mother.

Anyway, I got back together with Joanna again, and it was very good, great fun, but, like all the other relationships where I've been in love, it had a foreseeable future. People I have got involved with all had a certain span, one might be shortish, one might be longish, and with Joanna, it lasted six years.

I wasn't strong enough to actually say, Darling, I want to finish this. After six years it ain't that easy, but you give little hints. She left me a letter when I went on a skiing holiday on my own, and it said, 'You've hinted you are not happy, I have moved out . . .' What she thought would happen is that I would go and get her – and I didn't, so she was a bit unhappy, but I was brave enough to want to finish that relationship while I had nobody else at all, I just wanted out. I had a couple of odd girlfriends that summer, and then I met Deborah . . .

LYNDON

I have always had a problem about finding the women who I admire sexy, and the women I find sexy admirable. You meet a woman you really admire: she is intelligent, amusing, witty, attractive – so you stick your cock in her mouth . . .

We met when we were 18 years old on the first day of going to university; because our surnames had the same first four letters, we were sat next to each other in the language laboratory, and she was having difficulty fiddling around with this tape recorder, so I, with nauseous gallantry, offered to help her.

I thought she was just gorgeous – she looked like the young Elizabeth Taylor in *Cleopatra*, much the same eye make-up and beehive hair-do.

We were at a university where men and women were in the same college, and we were together all the time, so by the time we had been through university we were like an old married couple already, sex was no longer a particularly important part of our relationship, and indeed for many years I was quite convinced that you couldn't maintain a sexual relationship for any length of time, and that it didn't matter.

Women should complain more. Back in the sixties I think women were less honest, more likely to be complimentary to their men, and therefore less likely to get a decent result. If you insinuate to your man that you're having an entirely satisfactory sex life, you have only got to do it two or three times and you've locked in concrete the expectations for the next ten years or more, because if things are satisfactory, why should he change?

I think meeting people at 18 and entering on a sexual relationship you are doomed – you haven't a clue. I never had any complaints, I mean I was enthusiastic and I was considerate and imaginative, but I didn't really know what a woman enjoyed and what constituted an orgasm for a woman.

It wasn't until a relationship happened much later on in my life that I realised you could still be a wildly enthusiastic sexual partner to somebody you had been sleeping with for several years.

We intended when we left university to have a six-month break from one another, but never succeeded in doing so. I was already dubious about the extent to which I was happy in the relationship, but far too much of an emotional coward to do anything about it.

I remember getting married with the thought: I can always get divorced, it is not too bad a mistake.

I was first unfaithful to Mary after three years, when I went to the States on a business trip and I met an older woman of 28 – God, I would like to meet a woman of 28 now! – and suddenly I was exposed to exciting sex.

And then I was fairly regularly unfaithful; it is not a period of my life that I am particularly proud of, but I suppose I was sowing some oats that I hadn't sown earlier.

The women I tended to be unfaithful with were women who I could dominate. They tended to be people below me on a professional scale so it would be a secretary, or a junior partner, terribly improper really.

Mary found out a couple of times about it. I am deeply ashamed of it now, deeply ashamed of the hurt done to Mary.

It proved difficult for her to have a child, and that didn't help our sex life because we were bonking on monitor readings – she would be taking her temperature at regular times trying to find the moment when she ovulated, and at that moment we would have to have sex. Well, fourteen years into a relationship that ain't easy. Very often I would simply masturbate until such time as I was ready to come, and then I would insert the member and deposit the seed. In fact our child was born as a result of a voluntary and pleasant sexual act that took place on Boxing Day.

I was knocked out by the child whom I adored, but nonetheless within a year I was back to my old ways.

I admired Mary enormously, but I found her an undermining, somewhat castrating influence. She would undermine my enthusiasm for things, she would pooh-pooh my schemes.

Then I met the woman who really taught me about sex. She was like a sexual Disneyland really, she was gorgeous, she was tremendously active sexually, I mean she had a great sexual appetite. She is the only woman I have met whose sexual appetite is the same as mine: she wanted sex every day, and she got ratty if she didn't have it every day.

It was suddenly like being given a sex slave, toy, bimbo, who would do everything and was kind and gentle and loving and sexy, and it was just wonderful. I didn't admire her, like I had admired Mary, but I had a lovely, comfortable, sexy life, I couldn't resist it. It was irresistible. And I left Mary and established a relationship with this woman to whom I am now married.

I have always had a problem about finding the women who I admire sexy, and the women I find sexy admirable. You meet a woman you really admire: she is intelligent, amusing, witty, attractive – so you stick your cock in her mouth. That I think is partly from having gone to a boarding school where your first exposure to any kind of sexual experience is pornography, and you begin to separate women into categories.

SUZIE

I felt ashamed of myself for having been such a coward and . . . not being strong enough to stop the whole thing – even if it was on the morning of the wedding . . .

Sometimes I compare now with what it was like then, and I am very glad I got divorced; if we'd stuck it out I think I would have had to accept an awful lot of things that I didn't think were right, fundamental things that I think are the wrong way to do things, and I would have lost my self-respect in doing so.

We met at a party, and it was real sweep-you-off-your-feet business. That was New Year, 1977, and the summer of that year we went off for almost a year on a motor bike, and we went everywhere, Afghanistan, India, Africa.

Everyone says after doing a trip like that your relationship should be able to survive anything, but that's a load of baloney, because you are thrown together in situations where you have to get along, and you don't look at things that are beginning to go wrong . . .

I had inklings, occasions when I saw behaviour that I didn't like, the way he treated individuals we met and would make very instant friendships, and then drop them like hot bricks two days later, or he would make promises that he may well have intended to fulfil, but which he didn't, and I don't like that sort of attitude; it's very different from me, I take a long time to make friends, but then I will be friends with them for ever.

There was a lot of physical passion at first, and he seemed to have an outlook on life that I found attractive. He's a lawyer now, but, when I first started going out with him, he wanted to travel, he wanted to write, and he didn't seem terribly interested in making lots and lots of money. He seemed to be different from a lot of the other people that I knew who were staid professionals, chartered surveyors, doctors . . . lawyers.

And then, after we'd done our travelling, he appeared to change completely, well, that was my perception then, I mean it was probably there all the time, but he was in fact extremely ambitious, he wanted to make lots of money.

We came back from that trip in June, and we got married in the autumn, when what we should have been doing was splitting up. That's a classic thing: often when things are going wrong in relationships, neither party will face up to it, and will rush along another course of action – let's get married, or let's have a baby, or let's move house, and it stops you actually thinking about the relationship, because you get involved in all sorts of distractions.

I don't think I liked him, that's what was wrong, and I didn't have any respect for him; now I understand that that is fundamental to any relationship.

We got married on the 18th of October.

I knew I was making a horrendous mistake, but out of a mixture of stubbornness and reluctance to admit that I'd made a mistake, I wouldn't confess to it.

On the way down to the wedding, we stopped for a cup of coffee, and we had an enormous row in a café about something so stupid I can't even remember it, and I marched out of the car, and all I wanted to do was take my bag and go back to London. But I didn't, although I should have done.

We went to Tunisia on honeymoon, and, as I sat on the beach, I saw lots of happy people, or they appeared to be happy to me, and I felt so self-pitying and miserable sitting there, I just cried and cried. I didn't know what to do to get out of it, and I lacked the courage to say anything. So there was a tremendous feeling of helplessness, of hopelessness. I felt ashamed of myself for having been such a coward and not listening to my inner voice, and not being strong enough to stop the whole thing – even if it was on the morning of the wedding.

And the whole of the marriage, I never had the courage; we didn't talk about problems, we never sat down and tried to sort anything out, or discuss it in any way.

When we got back from honeymoon, we moved, which was a big mistake; we were living in a building site, it was just horrendous. You'd open the front door, and there was really no house, just walls and wires. There was nowhere you could sit down in peace and quiet, nowhere to read, it was very difficult to relax, and it was always terribly dirty, there was dust everywhere. Never let builders into your home – if you want the marriage to last.

Because we were so broke doing up the house, a friend of Robert's lived with us – I don't know if I fell in love with him, but I was extremely attracted to him, because he was the most divine-looking guy, an absolute sod, but very beautiful. I never did anything, but it was amazingly tempting. Robert was working long hours, and this man and I spent a lot of time together, we would even eat dinner in the evenings when Robert hadn't come home.

Very quickly we stopped having any sex at all, he was working such long hours that we were beginning to lead quite separate lives. But it was mutual in a way: as the relationship deteriorated, by unspoken agreement we kept away from each other, and on the weekends he was a sailing fanatic, or he had become a sailing fanatic, and my idea of pleasure wasn't scraping barnacles off a rusting hulk in a bitter east wind.

Eventually, we were spending so much time apart that even we couldn't ignore the fact that something was going dreadfully wrong. But instead of sitting down and saying, I am unhappy, and I am unhappy because of X, Y and Z, what should we do, I'd just express myself through ratty behaviour, and losing my temper, which was silly, it was helping no one: I was unhappy behaving like that, he was unhappy having a wife behaving like that – so we withdrew more and more.

And I can't remember exactly when it happened, but very calmly, one evening, I said I was going to move out – and even then we didn't discuss why, we just accepted that that was how it was going to be, and we went our separate ways.

A friend of mine had wanted someone to share his flat with him, and it was all very civilized, Robert drove me round there with my suitcase.

It was a tremendous feeling of relief, it was wonderful to be able to come and go as I pleased, and I felt very free and enormously glad that it was over, and I had finally done something instead of pushing it aside the whole time. And it did my self-respect some good because at least I felt as if I was taking some sort of control over my life. I think I would have gone crazy if we'd stayed together much longer.

Initially, if you are the person that leaves, you feel on a real high, and you zoom along for quite a while thinking life is wonderful; it was great to be able to go to bed when I wanted, to read my book when I wanted to, try on clothes at two in the morning if I wanted to, without this other person hissing over the bedclothes, 'Turn the bloody light off . . .'

But later, feelings of guilt, perhaps a sense of failure, do come into it.

And it made me very raw emotionally when I started having relationships with other people, because suddenly there you are in that whole field of emotions again, and you know you've screwed up one relationship very badly. So on the one hand it made me extremely cautious, and yet, on the other, I was very enthusiastic to have another go, I was looking forward to meeting someone. I hadn't had sex for so long that I was keen to prove to myself that I could actually do it again, I suppose I had started thinking there must be something wrong with me. I was relieved when someone found me attractive, and I hadn't completely shrivelled up, never to go out with anyone again.

I had an affair with someone six months after I split up with Robert, and when that finished I got terribly upset, really upset, and I lost an awful lot of weight, and looked an absolute wreck. I think that probably had more to do with my marriage failing than it had to do with the specific person, it churned up an awful lot of emotions.

But for the first time I really looked at myself and how my behaviour affected other people, and what I wanted out of a relationship, and I started taking more control over my own emotions.

I've learnt the importance of keeping lines of communication open, and that you don't sit and let things fester inside you: if you are unhappy with something, then you say you are – even if you are going to have a row, or the other person may be upset. I think it's far better to be honest and truthful, even if you cause a little bit of hurt in the process.

I had a horrendous time with my family. My mother felt there was a terrible stigma about divorce, no one in our immediate family had been divorced before, and for about six weeks she phoned me at the office every day, sobbing down the line. I didn't speak to my father for almost eighteen months – I went home after we'd split up, and he and I had an almighty row until about four in the morning, he could not understand how I could get divorced. He asked whether Robert was beating me, or had some sort of perverted sexual habit – he could have accepted it if there was something concrete like that. However, I still think his behaviour was appalling – he wrote me some horrible letters which we don't talk about now, but because of them I didn't speak to him for a long long time, and I didn't go home for two years.

Robert and I keep in touch; he had a Christmas party and I went to that, and he did my conveyancing for me. We don't search each other out in any way, but if we do see each other then we are perfectly amicable.

I would hope that anyone who has a divorce learns something from it. Without sounding pious, you damn well should. If you don't, you are just going to go round repeating the same mistakes.

RAY

In the ensuing struggle he half fell through the window, and jagged glass ripped open his back and shoulders, there was blood everywhere . . .

I had a little office in a mews in Soho, and I picked her up. She was a model, she used to come in regularly to her agency – she was and is devastating-looking. She is black, a bit black, her mother was Irish, she never knew her father.

And then one day she arrived carrying a rack of dresses, and I ran after her and said, 'Let me carry your things for you.' I made a date, and she didn't show up, but I persisted, I was just so devastated by the way she looked.

I thought she was the most wonderful thing in the world, I thought she was absolutely beautiful, she just touched me in a way that is beyond reasons. I was completely ensnared by this woman.

We had a baby before we married. I had a terrible ambivalence really, here is a nice middle-class boy coming down from the North of England to learn a good profession, and not only does he start living with a woman, not only does he have a baby out of wedlock, but for God's sake, she is black! I thought: Hey, what is happening here, babies, black girls, I was really shaking the bars of my predicted cage – and at all kinds of emotional levels I could not handle it. And I ran away to America, and then within a week I realised I couldn't get away, and so she came out to the States and we spent some time together, and finally we got married in Las Vegas. It was a gamble which didn't pay off.

She was still very much a teenager, very feckless, very wild, drinking a lot, doping a lot, a good mother, but erratic, and when we came back to England she went completely cuckoo, I mean sex and drugs and rock 'n' roll.

One evening she told me about two 'affairs': one was an affair, and the other was a squalid, drunken one-nighter. I was devastated but hey, fine, she was opening up and talking; I remember she was sitting on the sofa and I said, 'Stand up' – I wanted to put my arms round her, and she thought I was going to knock her over, she said, 'No, you will hit me.'

She didn't tell me about the third guy, and within a week I saw what was happening, she had confessed to two affairs to get them out of the way to start the third.

I was just in pieces, I couldn't work, emotionally I felt absolutely wrecked. I had put so much faith on this notion of the family, the couple, intimacy, togetherness, trust. I tried drink, I tried dope, above all I tried to talk, and she would duck and dive, she was just so evasive; the awful thing was that by then there were three kids, two girls and a boy, and she would go out every night, and I would look after the kids.

And then she said that she really wanted to end it with this guy and try to rebuild the marriage, and that it would be helpful if she could just go away one last time for the weekend.

I said yes . . . but the fact that he was there with the kids just killed me. I was alone in our house in London, and there was a broken desk, the leg had come off and was lying in a corner, and I picked it up, and I got into my car around 2 a.m., and I drove all the way to East Anglia, and somehow I found my way to this cottage. I think I was planning to smash in his car, but when I got there I was able to see inside one of the windows.

She was asleep with him in one room, the three kids were in the next bedroom. And that disgusted me, that is the thing that absolutely cracked me up. I broke into the house and started swinging at him with the table leg, caught him a couple of times on his head, I cracked open his skull – I can still remember the sound – and immediately he started to bleed. And when he got up and tried to defend himself, in the ensuing struggle he half fell through the window, and jagged glass ripped open his back and shoulders, there was blood everywhere. The kids were up, crying, anxious, we were making an awful noise.

She said, 'God, look at the mess, what are you going to do about the mess?' I said, 'Your mess, you can clear it up.'

I drove back, and the car broke down. I phoned the RAC, the RAC came to pick me up and I was covered in blood, the RAC thought I was the mad axeman and drove off. I hitchhiked back to London somehow and when I got back I found the police were all over the house. They were going to charge me with attempted murder, but finally it was GBH and assault. When it went to court I was discharged – the judge said I simply 'delivered a thrashing which he richly deserved'.

But I don't know if I ever recovered from that evening.

I became impotent, slowly, slowly, slowly. I went to see doctors, shrinks, hypnotherapists, acupuncturists, rebirthists, the whole thing for ten years.

I discovered I had multiple sclerosis and that's what caused it.

I was deteriorating rapidly, and she didn't much care. She behaved coldly towards me, I mean physically coldly: she was pleased to go on holiday, she was pleased to go out to dinner, pleased to be part of what the French call *le foyer*; if we were sitting at dinner she would hold my hand, touch me, but there would be limits on it, in bed, for example.

She went through a subsequent fourth affair with a gun-carrying criminal, a real East End hood, we're talking about injunctions, jail, police, beatings up, he was extremely violent.

Then, to cut an enormous and monstrous story short, finally I left, and the kids came with me, they couldn't stand living with her any longer, and she was by then deeply alcoholic and had become addicted to heroin.

The situation now is this; we are divorced, she has the oldest girl who is now 17, I have the two younger ones with me, and that's been the situation for six or seven years. She has been with AA for a couple of years, and has made great progress.

I see her because of the kids, we have Sunday dinner together, and she takes my breath away – I still, to this day, see something in her which is just devastating.

ANNE

In the morning I made that magnificent gesture you only ever see in the movies, which was to sweep the clothes out of the wardrobe, throw them in a suitcase and slam it shut – which gave me a great deal of satisfaction – and I then stood on the street and thought: Hmm, what next . . . ?

I come from an upper middle-class, intellectual, messy family, where everybody is either mad or an alcoholic or depressive, or went off having affairs, whereas Bill seemed to come from this family where everybody was ordinary and normal and manageable, and nobody had done anything outrageous. I think I wanted some security.

I remember at my wedding feeling I was very much in love and yet reassuring myself that one didn't absolutely have to stay with this person for ever, there was such a thing as divorce . . .

I find it very hard now to make statements about whether I was happy or not. There were lots of things wrong in our relationship; one thing was that Bill had one of those frightful male hangups about my previous sex life. It wasn't a case of what relationships I'd had, but who I'd been to bed with, and the fact that I had been to bed with other people before him. He couldn't cope with my not being a virgin, which was absurd. He wasn't. But he would get himself into a state of terrible anxiety about it, and the result of that was my not being allowed to acknowledge my past because it caused him such anguish.

And so I was constantly on guard, I would monitor the conversation with friends, make sure if I saw anything coming I could stop it, because I'd see Bill stiffening into a state of agitation, and I knew he was going to be terribly depressed afterwards.

I had had two real sexual relationships. I'd had a boyfriend in my last year at school, quite a strong relationship, I know him still, and we exchanged passionate letters for a while. But under supervision from Bill, I burnt diaries, photograph albums, letters . . . can you believe it?

I remember feeling bored, that I actually couldn't be bothered with this, it was too stupid.

I guess it was a pretty dishonest relationship, I don't think we confronted a lot of things that mattered. The day to day existence was sort of all right, but our lives were very much looking outwards, we spent very little time alone, we were very busy socially and both working quite hard, and in the evenings we'd go out with other people.

And we never discussed our relationship. I think we were scared of confronting anything too personal, and I was sufficiently insecure that I wanted this relationship to continue rather than strike out on my own.

Bill had to go away on business, during which time I didn't have a period, and I had a pregnancy test which was positive, and I felt more strongly than I had ever felt about anything in my life that I did not want to have that child, and I knew at that point Bill was not the person I wanted to spend the rest of my life with.

I went off to have an abortion.

Around that time a solicitor arrived at my firm who was a kindred spirit, not a grey, City type like most of them, and we got on very well, we would have lunch together two, three times a week. We were terribly good friends, we had matters to talk about. And then one day our hands met, and next thing, we were having a passionate embrace across the restaurant table, and I remember leaving, and feeling slightly stunned, and having this awful, wonderful conversation afterwards, 'What's going on . . . ?' That was very exciting.

And in a fairly short space of time we realised we were going to have to go to bed together, and working out the logistics of that. He and his wife had bought a new house, without having sold the old one – which gave us a place to go.

Sex with Mark was absolutely wonderful. And one of the things that was so wonderful was the fact that we talked about it, all the time, particularly when we were making love. I could tell him what I wanted. I realised then how frightened Bill and I had been about discussing sex.

Bill's antennae, which had been so sensitive when it came to long-past relationships, were absolutely hopeless. I remember Mark and I were walking back from lunch and we bumped into Bill, and we obviously handled it terribly well, because he just didn't realise. It was only the past he was suspicious about.

Mark and I began plotting to run away together, we talked about it for ages. His marriage had been frightful, his wife had become fantastically fat, unbelievably, unacceptably overweight, and he'd had no sex life at all.

And then this wonderful thing happened. I wanted a cigarette and I couldn't find a light, and I went to look in Bill's briefcase for some matches, and there was this letter lying open – waiting to be read – and it was from somebody he worked with, with whom he was clearly having an affair. And so I read this letter, this stupid letter, which was probably no more stupid than the letters I was writing to Mark, challenging him about some occasion when they'd been supposed to meet and he hadn't met her, and about her feeling jealous of me, and an awful lot about how much she loved him. And I remember a wonderful sense of elation, an overwhelming sense of joy, I didn't need to feel guilty any more, this was my absolution.

One evening we were getting into bed and Bill started pulling back the sheets and looking at them, and I realised something was up, and it turned out he had followed me and Mark; we had had a cup of tea in a local café and we'd then kissed each other goodbye.

He had no proof I had slept with Mark but he had decided that was the case. He asked me if I'd slept with him, and I didn't deny anything. He asked me what I wanted to do, and I said I wanted to live with Mark, and he was incredibly upset and angry, and told me to get out.

I was perfectly willing to go, and I stayed the night on the sofa in the sitting-room, and in the morning I made that magnificent gesture you only ever see in the movies, which was to sweep the clothes out of the wardrobe, throw them in a suitcase and slam it shut – which gave me a great deal of satisfaction – and I then stood on the street and thought: Hmm, what next . . . ?

I sat outside my sister's office with my suitcase, trying to look as nonchalant as possible, and when Susan appeared she gave me the keys to her flat, and I took my suitcase there, got changed and went to the office.

I told Mark what had happened, and about a week later he told his wife about me – and then Mark and I were both homeless. Within a few days Bill was knocking on my door and wanting me to come back, desperately wanting me back. 'It's not a serious relationship,' he said, 'it's a flippant affair, *we've* got so much . . .'

For the first time I was actually confronting the break-up of this marriage, and so I was in a highly emotional state, I was spending all the time in tears. Bill put me under very severe emotional pressure, and I agreed to come back, but I extracted a promise out of him that I had to be allowed to remain friends with Mark, which was absurd, that's how much unreality was going down. Even more absurd, Bill agreed to it. Anyway, I went back to Sue's, and then thought: This is ridiculous, the last thing I want to do is go back to Bill, and so I rang him, and canned the deal.

Mark meanwhile was dealing with a very unhappy wife who was doing the if-you-don't-come-around-this-minute-I'm-going-to-commit-suicide number on him, but in amongst it, somehow Mark and I still had a relationship, were still desperately in love with each other.

I rang Bill and said I thought we ought to get divorced, and he was very resistant about it, but eventually he did agree. It took two years.

I was on my way to the office and this letter came through the post, and I remember seeing the words 'Decree Absolute', and I sat down on the stairs and burst into floods of tears, and felt absolutely desolate for a few hours, completely desolate. I remember saying to myself: It's not that I want the relationship back, don't get confused, but it's a bit like when somebody dies, you often weep most at the funeral. I remember when my father died, it wasn't until I realised he was inside the coffin that I really understood he was dead.

IONA

He wanted to marry me and I didn't really mind, but not really minding is not a particularly brilliant reason for going into a marriage . . .

I thought the sun shone: there was a 29-year-old publisher who knew about all these fascinating things, and here was this little 18-year-old student who knew bugger all about anything, and I just sat and thought: Ah, his brains, his brilliance; his ideas and his friends were more interesting than mine, and I threw all my personal luggage out of the window and adopted his.

We'd had a gay friend for dinner one night who said, 'One day you will do the sensible thing and settle down together,' and when he left I said, 'Surely, the last person on God's planet trying to make us do the straight thing would be Ted.' 'Perhaps he is right,' said Henry. 'Is that a proposal?' I said. 'Suppose so,' said Henry.

After he proposed I didn't have the courage to say I thought I had made a mistake.

We drove down to Corfu in his open-top sports car, and I spent a lot of time trying to find a way to say I had made a mistake, but it is very difficult to have a conversation in an open-top car at 110 m.p.h. on the Autostrada, and when we got to Corfu there was a nice house party and lots of jolly people, and I relaxed and thought: Well, fuck it, it can't be that bad. He wanted to marry me and I didn't really mind, but not really minding is not a particularly brilliant reason for going into a marriage.

Getting married is an organisational feat. I like organisational challenges, it is like a bone to a dog. I am a nicely brought-up English girl, if somebody says this is how it is done, dear, you do your damnedest to do it like that. I just got on and did it.

Our honeymoon was a complete nonstarter. We went to the

Dordogne and Henry developed a chronic earache, and it was over Easter and we couldn't find a doctor; I got desperate curse pains and came back with an infection and had to have my coil out – and that is how Joanna slipped round the home straight and lodged herself firmly in place.

Henry was brilliant while I was pregnant, and terribly sympathetic. I was actually very pleased to be pregnant even though I hadn't planned on having a child that early, and the doubts I had before sort of melted away.

But after I had William, I was stitched up the wrong way and felt thoroughly miserable and off sex, and obviously too much rejection from me didn't help, so he then felt disinclined.

Bed never got any better, two small children, lots and lots of entertaining, and we would always go and stay with his parents at weekends; I think we had dinner alone together about nine times in the first three years of marriage, which with hindsight is not a particularly brilliant way of conducting a marriage.

And finally, I suppose predictably, I fell into the arms of somebody who was equally frustrated, and I had an affair with him which was almost safe because he wasn't going to leave his wife, and I didn't want to leave Henry because the children were too small, so it seemed a reasonable solution. He was highly intelligent and extremely interesting and taught me an awful lot about business, and he was very reassuring, and gave me a lot of self-confidence.

I was extremely good at adultery because I am so organised, I managed to make spaces in days that shouldn't have had spaces in them. And I picked up a second wind from the new relationship and I became completely obsessed about this guy, I couldn't give him up at all. I kept on trying because I knew it was the wrong thing to be doing, but I just couldn't, and certainly in the early stages I would have run off with him, given the opportunity, although I very carefully made sure there was no opportunity.

Of course it unravelled what was left of my relationship with Henry, and I became very tense and increasingly unhappy with him. Whether Henry knew or didn't know I was having an affair is a pretty moot point. I think he had extremely strong suspicions which he chose not to air because it would have been incredibly destructive to have aired them.

And then one day I'd had a row with this guy, and he decided to pour his undying love on a piece of paper – I think he realised things were coming to a close and I was backing off. So from somebody who up until then had only written thirteen columns of figures that cross-balanced beautifully, here was suddenly a love letter, which is the last thing you need when you are sitting in bed with your husband. He had dropped it through the letter box and the au pair brought it up. I screwed it up, put it on the bedside table, husband lay awake all night waiting to read it, I lay awake all night waiting to throw it away, it was dreadful. The next morning he said, 'What was all that about?' and I said, 'Well, you can't be oblivious of the fact that this guy and I are very fond of each other . . .' 'Oh, but have you slept with him?' I've always thought lies are the best policy and said, 'No, I haven't,' but that really wasn't going to hold up very long. In the end I was supposed to make up my mind as to which one I wanted. Ghastly. The answer was neither of them but I couldn't work that one out either, so I just jacked in the lover.

I turned up one day and said, 'If you want to run away with me run away with me now,' and he said, 'I'll have to go home and tell my wife,' so I said, 'Forget it, bye, bye.' I struggled along with Henry for another year getting more and more stressed; it was quite amicable, we were just unable to exchange words. Black for me was white for him, and vice versa, we could have been talking a foreign language – which would have been easier because we could have used a dictionary.

I was very sad when Henry moved out. I wish we could have found a solution where we could have gone on living together, but we just couldn't.

I then went back to the lover for another six months, although I knew that was a mistake from the word go.

He had rung up one day and said, 'I am going to Paris on business, why don't you come too.' So I said, 'No bonking and Le Crillon or I am not coming.' I'm horrible. So that night we stayed at Le Crillon, and by the time you have had a bottle of wine at dinner, and there is nothing better to do, and there is nobody else in your life anyway . . .

I worked out that I actually didn't need to go on thinking about Henry, we weren't going to get back together again. I didn't even want to, if I was honest, although the children lean on you very heavily to get back together. But we still speak on the telephone, a sort of who-is-collecting-the-children-from-X-and-Y, but we find excuses to speak to each other, and when we are pissed off we ring each other up and grumble, but I think that is gradually going away.

If you are a child of divorced parents it makes it much easier to be divorced, the whole mechanics of the thing become easier. My mother has been divorced four times – I know that handover time for children is an emotional nightmare, and causes people to have nervous breakdowns; when a child comes back minus its knickers, its best shoes and its party dress which it has to wear the following Tuesday evening, I just take a big deep breath. And if you say you will drop them back at six you drop them back at six on the dot, not five minutes before and not five minutes after. I know all that.

The man I am now living with used to be my next-door neighbour. Someone said, 'You don't go far to get laid, do you?' I had what I thought was going to be a six-week fling, but it is still fun, so a year on I am still flinging.

ANGUS

We went on the most disastrous honeymoon of all time . . . where I have a feeling the affair which ended the marriage started . . .

I met her at a nurses' dance, she was a nurse at Somerset General Hospital, and we started an affair. She was a virgin, and she fell deeply in love. I am not sure that I did, maybe I did, I don't know. But she was extremely neurotic and nervous about it all because of her parents.

Her father was an NCO in the RAF, and he thought I was some dreadful person spoiling his young daughter. He had several daughters but she was the one who had succeeded, she won the gold medal for nursing and was top of all the nursing classes, and she was the apple of his eye, the one who was best of all.

And the apple of his eye was not going to go to somebody who he didn't approve of in every conceivable way. He'd much rather some promising young man from the services had taken her up, not some fucking pseudo-intellectual and frightfully, frightfully journalist.

I was a different class from him, for one thing; she came from a lower middle-class milieu and I come from upper middle-class Scottish lairdery, and I have this kind of BBC speaking voice and she had a Somerset accent, and he was deeply suspicious of intellectuals like myself doing the dirty on his daughter. He was out of his class, out of his depth, he was one of those people who deeply suspected anybody who dared to be artistic or was well educated. Eton and Oxford seemed well out of his league, he sort of admired it, but he deeply resented it too.

I can remember it all culminated in a fearful letter from him full of incestuous jealousy, saying, 'Hands off my daughter, you filthy, lecherous bastard: if you soil my daughter . . .' It was the most astonishing and abnormal letter.

After about three years we decided to get married, whereupon, after an enormous row with the father, he sort of accepted me and there was a marriage in Yeovil. But even as I walked up the aisle I thought: I am not sure whether we should be getting married or parting.

I am sure that an enormous number of people get married because their relationship is not going well and they think that this will make it OK – and it doesn't.

Sexually it was terrible between us, we were just not very interested in each other any more.

And we went on the most disastrous honeymoon of all time to Spain where I have a feeling the affair which ended the marriage started: a friend of mine came along for part of the time, and he probably had an affair with her under my very nose during our honeymoon . . .

Within even a few weeks, certainly a few months, the marriage was really a wreck; we were extremely fond of each other, but she had transferred herself sexually to this other man.

She began to take drugs from the hospital cupboards, morphine and things like that, and she started drinking quite heavily . . . eventually she became a full-blown alcoholic, at the age of not much more than 25.

We both knew that the marriage was at an end . . . She went off with this man, who made her deeply unhappy, he was of course married and he really couldn't give the enormous support such a vulnerable and neurotic person needed, and she sank further into the depths of alcoholism, and things went from bad to worse because he wasn't prepared to leave his wife. She was deeply unhappy about that, and she was deeply unhappy about me because she still sort of loved me and felt enormous guilt about me. It was one of those dreadful messes that human beings get themselves into.

The divorce itself was terribly simple. The only simple thing about our relationship was the divorce. Isn't it strange that one can have a deeply neurotic and strange relationship, and yet the divorce which could have been the worst thing, ought to have been the worst thing, was the easiest and least traumatic event in our marriage?

Unfortunately, what I haven't told you is that, by the time I left her, she had got pregnant and had a child. Whether the child was mine or his is a moot point which I will never discover, and nor will he; she's my daughter now, she regards me as her father, and I may very well be her father. But I thought: *I* will be father to the child, because I'm sure this other chap's not going to be – and I always have been, and it's a very good relationship.

One day at my office my secretary took a phone call, and said, 'Oh Angus, I've got some bad news for you, your wife is dead.' She was my ex-wife by then, of course, and I just thought: Oh my God, she has committed suicide.

But I can remember feeling very little emotion, I thought: What a relief, because she was destroying herself anyway, and at least the daughter was now safe from that awful influence; she was a good mother in many ways, but if you're a drunk you're never really a good mother.

The funny thing was, because she became an alcoholic, her fucking father rejected her, and began to think of me as an awfully decent chap who had stood by her and who had always looked after my daughter – and instead of hating me like he used to, he had enormous admiration for me.

And I can remember sitting in the taxi going to the funeral; by that time the father had got out of the RAF, and he was, believe it or not, a social services man. He was talking frightful fascist crap: 'Those are the blocks of flats I have to go to, frankly, I'd burn them, and all the people in them too.' On his way to his daughter's funeral, for fuck's sake! 'I don't know why I'm going to this funeral, she's let us all down, she's proved to be absolutely nothing, but *you've* been marvellous . . .'

LUCY

He looked absolutely gorgeous that night, he was in his black tie standing at the top of the stairs, so he looked a bit taller than he really is, and he was attractively unshaven – but not in that disgusting tramplike way he is now, and he was being very witty because he was slightly tiddly, but not pissed out of his brains, which he subsequently became so often . . .

I had been going out with Timothy on and off for about eight years; whenever it was on we didn't really get on very well, but whenever it was off we missed each other, and would begin going out together again. What I missed about Timothy when I wasn't with him was the ability to be really familiar with someone. I respected his talent, he is a brilliant architect, and loved talking to him about it; sex was good because it was familiar, although it wasn't anything fantastic. I also thought he was one of the most beautiful people I knew, and I just loved looking at him. But it was a masochistic relationship because we made each other quite miserable, and whenever I had got a new boyfriend I would always get lured back to Timothy and break the other person's heart – that sounds terribly conceited, but I mucked a few people about as a result of it.

But I had got to an age and stage where I felt ready to get married, and I really wanted to get rid of that ball and chain. I met Neil at a dinner party, and he was the first man for a very long time who I thought was truly beautiful to look at. He looked absolutely gorgeous that night, he was in his black tie standing at the top of the stairs, so he looked a bit taller than he really is, and he was attractively unshaven – but not in that disgusting tramplike way he is now, and he was being very witty because he was slightly tiddly, but not pissed out of his brains, which he subsequently became so often. I didn't know anyone at this party, I'd been taken by my business partner Jeremy, who is a very nice but very straight banker, and everyone there was very serious and polite and tame. Neil kept saying what I thought were really amusing things, and I cracked up laughing, which, as no one else did, made it even more funny. So I thought he was wonderful. He proceeded to get very drunk, which as he wasn't my escort didn't really worry me, and in fact he was lying on the floor when I left.

Neil had asked me for my telephone number during the course of the evening, and I had given it to him, and he then rang me up the next day and asked me out to supper. He turned up reeking of alcohol, very dirty and unshaven, with his huge hairy dog that ran amok in my little Kensington flat. I disliked him immediately, and thought: What a jerk. I was sure he was over the limit when he drove me to the restaurant, which turned out to be a grotty hamburger joint, he hadn't booked anywhere, and he was really rude to the waitress.

I had actually been out to dinner with a different man every night that week, and they all had BMWs, so there was some charm about the fact that Neil was different from them, and all the other yuppies I had met, at least he was unusual, and we had quite a provocative conversation about life. He came in for a cup of black coffee which I felt I should give him because he was never going to get home like he was. He asked if he could stay on the sofa, and I said no, I knew that whole thing of wandering into your bedroom as soon as the lights are off, it's a sort of poor man's move really: not bold enough to ask to sleep with you, and not daring enough to make a pass. I just wanted him out of my life and my flat and everything. And, when he asked if he could see me again, I said, 'No, I think you are pretty unpleasant,' and I meant it.

And then next day at work, I got the most massive bunch of flowers, and I got them every single day for a week, and they were really gorgeous, and I thought: Well, he must be very rich – which was completely wrong, but lovely to think. There is something about flowers . . . I know it is corny. And then he rang me to see if I had got the flowers, and I thanked him, 'But unfortunately it hasn't changed my mind about the way you behaved the other evening.' And he absolutely begged to see me one more time: could I give him another chance? And he was so sorry and pleading, I said, 'Well, provided you are sober and clean and it is during the daytime,' and he said, 'Fine.'

And when he came to pick me up he was actually shaking with nerves. But he was sober and clean – and very nice, a much nicer person because he wasn't drunk. He had booked a beautiful restaurant in the country, and it was a really romantic day, and I felt warm towards him, and found him very attractive as well. He suggested we stay down there, which I declined, but I agreed to dinner the following week.

And he was nice again, he seemed very sweet, and I went to bed with him, I wanted it to happen, which is why it happened.

The next day it was as if nothing had happened because I wasn't really in love with him yet, and I found myself in a very familiar situation, which was a Friday night in the pub with Timothy Brown, and another familiar situation, that he came back to my flat. I had just got into bed with him when the phone rang, and it was Neil. He said, 'I really, really love you, I think you are the most wonderful person in the world,' and I was just so delighted with this – and there was boring bloody Timothy Brown in my bed snoring and farting away, I can't even remember if I had bonked him or not. He just said, 'Who is that? Is that one of your lovers?' Neil then said, 'I'm coming round to see you,' and I said, 'Er, actually, don't, I have got a headache, and I am terribly tired . . .' I couldn't say, There is another man in the very bed you were in the other night. But after I put the phone down I felt so mean that I had hurt Neil, and that in a way he was the better person, that I made Timothy get up and get dressed, and I drove to Neil's flat in Clapham, and stayed with him, and we then saw each other every day after that.

The first three months were absolute heaven but totally irresponsible. We did crazy things like staying in bed for three days, we threw caution to the wind. For me being irresponsible meant not going to work and getting up really late and not having to go to dinner parties, but I was also making regular calls to work to make sure things were running smoothly, and going in on the odd day. I thought Neil was doing the same thing. But he wasn't, he was literally never ringing up work and not telling anyone where he was, he was being very irresponsible. We went off on a skiing holiday in February, and when we got back his company had gone into liquidation, he hadn't been in control at all, and I began to lose respect for him because he had left all his poor men working away, and hadn't rung them or been concerned about them in any way.

Nevertheless, November, December and January were heaven, lots of sex, and fun, and he told me his divorce would be through in January. And as I was totally and utterly in love with him I was relaxed about contraception, and I got pregnant at the end of January. We found out together, we did one of those tests. We were delighted, it was really romantic and wonderful, and I just thought it was magical this could happen to me. But I started to become very serious, which is what I am really like anyway, asking questions like when will his divorce be through, if he had written to so and so, where would we live, and what would we do – and that is when I found out about his company being liquidated at more or less the same time. And I suddenly began to hate him, I hated the fact that he chain-smoked, and I hated his dog, and millions of other things, and I had terrible morning sickness all the time, and I didn't want to have this baby because I didn't want to be tied to Neil for ever, because even if we didn't get married he would come and visit for the rest of my life. So I had an abortion which he didn't want me to have. But he was very sweet, and came with me, and said, 'Well, OK, it's your decision.'

I didn't realise how that would affect me, but it made me incredibly depressed and regretful: Oh my God, the first time I've met someone who I really did think was wonderful, I have done this to him. And that made me want to marry him again and have children and try to make things nice again.

But by the time his divorce came though in August, the whole romance of the thing had gone, and marriage was a thing we had to do because we had planned to do it for so long.

We got married at Christmas. The wedding itself was great; the honeymoon wasn't so great, I felt really depressed a lot of the time, I was homesick, there were no friends around or Christmas presents, and it was a long one, a month. And also I think I suddenly realised what I had done with Timothy Brown, suddenly I'd put a brick wall between us, and I would never ever be able to see or sleep with him, and I felt really upset about that. We went to Aspen, skiing, which was a surprise for me because I hadn't been told where we were going – I would have liked to have gone somewhere hot. In fact when we got to Aspen, I bought tickets to Miami for the last two weeks, because a month is an awfully long time to ski, it isn't romantic or sexy: when you go on honeymoon you should have lots of lovely silk lingerie and wear pretty dresses and things, and we had to wear long johns day in and day out. And also I imagined on honeymoon you just don't want to leave your hotel room or anything, and sex was OK, but it wasn't very often, partly because he was so exhausted with skiing.

When we came back we threw ourselves into the marriage and things related to it, like doing up the flat and having dinner parties and opening up wedding presents, and getting the photos done, and all that was fun because I love being incredibly busy. I got pregnant again in February, so that was another excitement. And then I had a miscarriage in April, and that was a disappointment, but in a funny kind of way a part of me felt relieved as well.

Living with Neil had become more and more stressful and I had cause to nag him, I felt, and I did.

Things like communication. He hates the phone. He would never ring me and say when he was coming home from work, if he was going to be late. It sounds so awfully clichéd, but I would go home, and I had worked really hard myself, and he just wouldn't come home for hours and hours, he would have gone to the pub straight after work and not told me. He doesn't drink very often but when he does he drinks very heavily, so there were lots of rows when he would come home at eleven, drunk, and I had been sitting there with his supper since seven.

He would say, 'Don't be such a boring nag, I am not joined to you at the hip,' and I would say, 'Fair enough, but neither am I your slave.'

We would never go out to a restaurant, and I found that very depressing, unglamorous and unromantic; we never had any cause to dress up to be with each other, and any element of romance was just being eaten away.

Neil very rarely initiated sex, he was pretty lazy about it, and he was always totally and absolutely and utterly exhausted because he was doing a lot of physical work in the day, and the evenings when he was home he was plastering walls, painting, stripping, replumbing, rewiring.

The other great strain on our marriage was he employed a team of builders, and, whenever one of them didn't have work to do, Neil would send him round to the flat to do a job. But he would never tell me, he would just give them keys, and I would be wandering round in the nude or something, and some tatty man with eight fags in his mouth would come wading in grunting, and start doing something in the flat. I absolutely couldn't bear that, and I would have big rows with Neil about it, and he would say, 'You want the flat done, don't you?'

So we battled on. In August I got pregnant again. By this stage things were very stressful between us, in every single aspect of our lives there seemed to be stress. I had another miscarriage in September, and I became really angry, I suddenly realised that in a year I had been through three pregnancies, his first divorce, his liquidation and another imminent liquidation of the second company. And I had moved from a very nice flat in Kensington to a building site in Clapham, and had become a drudge and a house cleaner. I was angry, I felt I had given away all the good things I had had, and was not getting any of the good things back I had thought I would get from marriage. And I began to hate him.

By the time Christmas came it was fairly clear that his business was going into liquidation for a second time, and it was also clear that he was avoiding the issue by not answering his mail or even opening it, nor bothering to get phones reconnected. I started to open his mail, because I got pretty worried about what was going on. The first letter was from the mortgage company saying they were going to repossess the flat because he hadn't paid the mortgage for many months, which baffled me because we had a joint bank account, and I had been putting all my money in it.

By that stage I really hated him, and yet I couldn't quite bring myself to walk away – there is something about me which makes me really want to make things work. And I am very sentimental, I opened a cupboard and found the top layer of our wedding cake, which should have been a christening cake, then there were all the wedding photographs everywhere, I would see wedding presents from relatives who had known me since I was a child, and I just couldn't bear to let them know. And also, there was the added fear of being single again. Because I wanted to be married and have children in my life, my next stepping stone after having separated from Neil would have been to try and find someone else to do all those things with, and I really couldn't face going through that whole dating scene again, trying to find someone who might turn out to be even worse.

I moved out for a few weeks.

I had refused to see Timothy after I got married, because if I am honest I still felt quite a lot for him. I was worried about the effect he would have on me, because he had always succeeded in luring me back to him from other men before. So I didn't see him, but I spent a lot of time thinking about Timothy Brown and wishing that I was with him and wondering what he was doing, and really became obsessed by it. And the worse things were with Neil the more I romanticised about how things had been with Timothy.

And when I moved out from Neil I met Timothy Brown in a pub for lunch. It was like a film, I walked in the pub and he was sitting down facing a log fire, and he turned around, and I still had the same butterfly thing in my stomach that I always had, and he was absolutely enchanting and wonderful and nice. We discussed everything very platonically and sweetly, and he took me back to his flat where he cooked lamb chops and potatoes in the middle of the day – he lives off school-dinner-type food, it was sweet, and he then settled down to watch the rugby. A few days later I went out to dinner with Timothy, and he was much less of a friend then. He came in to collect me, he kissed me hello, and he tried to grab me at the same time; then after supper he came in for a cup of coffee, and it was a real wrestling match. He wanted to go to bed with me, and I just did not feel like doing that – with him, or Neil, or anyone. And he got aggressive and nasty, and in the end I was disgusted by his behaviour, and I went right off him, and haven't missed him or thought about him since.

I went back to Neil. We were sharing a bed, but once or twice a week we had such a bad row that Neil would sleep in the spare room; the reason he didn't do that every night is that our bed is infinitely more comfortable than the spare-room bed, and it was also very big, big enough not to have to touch each other at all, which we didn't. And within a month I moved out for good.

My wish is that somebody would come along, another man, with whom I would just fall hopelessly in love, and vice versa, and he would transfer me from the situation I am in now.

He would be very reliable, very safe, very steady, he would have to be very good-looking, very sexy and great fun, and he would also be solvent and honest. He doesn't exist, I know many men like that, and they are just incredibly dull and, if he was all those things, he really wouldn't want to go out with a short, fat, half-divorced 34 year old, and I feel very depressed about it. I feel I have done a lot of damage to myself emotionally in the last couple of years, there is an awful lot of scarring there which might have made me incapable of having a normal relationship with somebody else.

JEAN

I saw his nieces . . . and I got such a shock that I just stood there and stared at them . . . I was horrified, I thought: What happens if our children turn out with brown skin?. . .

I met David Miller at the St James's Ball – it was very romantic.

He called me at work the next day and I couldn't see him because we were working on a very big deal, I couldn't even speak to him on the telephone.

He came round to the office the next day and I still couldn't see him because of this merger deal, and he waited downstairs for three hours, and the security men were getting more and more irate. So I went downstairs, and I was actually quite shocked when I saw him, he seemed very dark, he had a lot of facial hair, a big six o'clock shadow, and was just not at all how I remembered him. I suppose he looked a bit foreign.

But we arranged to meet later that night, and he must have just shaved, and I thought he was very handsome again. And we went off to a night club and stayed until three o'clock, and danced the last dance. And then he walked me home, it was pouring with rain outside, and we walked along Bond Street chatting all the way, and he told me about his ex-girlfriends and I told him about my ex-boyfriends, and we discussed music, and he told me he was a composer and that he was writing a film score, and I love music, it's a great part of my life.

He phoned me the moment I got into the office the next day and took me out to lunch, and from then on we met every lunchtime, and he took me out every evening, and wined and dined me and fed me champagne and took me to wonderful restaurants, and was really attentive and caring, and I was just swept off my feet.

I didn't want to sleep with him immediately because I wanted the first time to be special. One day he took me to a tree in Hampton Court where he said he spent a lot of time composing lyrics and music, and that is where it happened, on the grass. I felt rather sad because I wanted to be in a comfortable place, I didn't want to be on the ground getting all mucky.

But I loved that he was with me all the time, I loved that he saw me every lunchtime, I loved that he bought me presents. I was completely bowled over.

We set a weekend to go up to Yorkshire so he could meet my parents and ask Daddy if he could marry me, to do it the proper English way – David was into that sort of thing.

David gets on very well with his mother and we arranged to meet her for tea at the Carlton Tower, and as we were walking there he said, 'Look, there is something I need to tell you about my mother,' and I wondered what could possibly be a problem, because he had spoken about her in such a loving way. And he said, 'She is half French.' I thought: That's not a problem, I think the French are wonderful. And of course I didn't find out what the other half was, I just assumed she was half French and half English. And when I met her I was quite shocked by her appearance, she was petite and very chic, but she looked foreign, there was no doubt about it.

We had our official engagement party at Annabel's and that is when I met all his family. Again I was surprised. They weren't as English as I thought they were going to be. David had said he was born in Surrey, and that he had gone to Eton and Cambridge and had worked in the City, so I thought: Oh, very English. My father got chatting to David's father and I overheard David's father saying something about being born in the Middle East, and I thought: That's odd, but I didn't let it bother me.

Then a real crisis came when I met his two nieces, who were his sister's children.

I went to his sister's house, a beautiful house in Mayfair, and I saw his nieces, and they had very brown skin, and I got such a shock that I just stood there and stared at them. I felt: My God, what am I doing? I always had this image that I would marry an Englishman, who had probably been to Eton and Cambridge and worked in the City, and David had seemed to personify my expectations. But I looked at these two girls and I was horrified, I thought: What happens if our children turn out with brown skin?

We went out for supper and I was very quiet, and David said, 'What is the matter?' I couldn't say, Look, I thought you were English, I don't want to marry you because I am scared our children will turn out with brown skins . That is really what I wanted to say, but I knew it would hurt him too much. He tried so hard to be the English gentleman.

I even remember saying to him before I met his family, 'I hate these bloody Arabs, they have bought all the beautiful houses that used to belong to English people,' and I suppose that is a bit racist, but I just don't like Arabs.

I got on the phone to my parents and I said, 'I have just met his nieces and they are brown, what do I do?' And Mummy said, 'Don't worry, I am sure your children won't look like that because David is very pale, I'm sure he's English,' and Daddy was saying, 'You shouldn't let this stand in the way if you love him; it doesn't matter what colour somebody's skin is.' And I thought: Well, perhaps it is nasty of me to break it off just because he is not English.

And I talked to David and he assured me he was perfectly English. So I said to him, 'I was just a bit concerned about your nieces because they appeared so brown, and I was worried our children would have funny-coloured skin.' He looked very hurt, and I said, 'It doesn't matter, I love you, it doesn't matter.'

David didn't ever seem to work, but there was plenty of money at first, his parents gave him a very generous allowance, and if ever we needed more he would just go to his mother and she would hand it out to him. But things started getting really difficult when his father told her she must not give him any money: 'He is going to be married,' he said, 'he has to stand on his own two feet.'

The wedding day rolled ever closer and things began to go badly wrong. My wedding dress was ordered, it was going to cost a fortune, and of course he couldn't afford it when his parents' money was cut off. I ended up having to go to Laura Ashley and choose one of their cotton dresses, it wasn't the silk number I planned on having, and I was a bit upset about that.

We'd been to Hatton Garden and chosen the ring, sapphires and diamonds in a traditional setting, and he couldn't afford that either, so his mother had to give me one of her rings, and I was desperately disappointed, it was ugly and it was modern, and I hated it.

We didn't have a honeymoon. He had said we were going to go

round the world – we had chosen our route, but of course there was no money.

It was just after we'd been married a month that I found out he had not been to Cambridge. He had said he got a first in modern languages at Magdalene, but my sister was convinced he was lying to me, so she phoned up Cambridge and asked,'Have you heard of David Miller?' and she phoned me up and said, 'David Miller did not go to Cambridge.' I asked David about that and he said, 'I think I had better tell you, that is not my real name.' I was horrified – his name wasn't David Miller at all, it was something else, an Arabic name, and he had changed his name by deed poll just before we got married. My sister then phoned Cambridge again and said, 'Have you heard of *this* chap?' and they said no, and eventually he admitted he hadn't been to Cambridge. I did not know what to say. We had talked about Cambridge so much together.

And he hadn't been to Eton, of course. And there was no job in the City. He hadn't written a film score. I tried so hard not to get angry with him, not to feel disappointment. But everything was just completely fabricated. And I found out he didn't have a British passport, he actually had a Jordanian passport – and his leave to stay had expired about five years ago and he was living in this country as an illegal alien. Of course we could never have gone on honeymoon abroad, because if we had left the country he would never have been allowed back in.

I hated him for lying to me, I felt really cheated, he had married me under false pretences. He lied on our marriage certificate: he had put the wrong date of birth, the wrong nationality, even the wrong name, I mean it was all false, one thing after another. I just couldn't cope with it, I left at Christmas.

A NOTE ON THE AUTHOR

Lost Hearts confirms Danny Danziger's place as one of the best interviewers in the country. He has a weekly column in the *Independent*, and his previous books include *The Happiness Book*, *All in a Day's Work*, *Eton Voices*, *The Cathedral*, and *The Noble Tradition*.